İstanbul 1435 / 2014

THE ISLAMIC APPROACH TO
REASON AND PHILOSOPHY

Original Title:	İslam Nazarında Akıl ve Felsefe
Author :	Osman Nuri Topbaş
Translator :	Fulya Vatansever
Redactor :	Süleyman Derin
Graphics :	Cihangir Taşdemir
Printed by :	Erkam Printhouse
ISBN :	978-9944-83-662-3
Address :	Ikitelli Organize Sanayi Bölgesi Mah. Atatürk Bulvarı, Haseyad 1. Kısım No: 60/3-C Başakşehir, Istanbul, Turkey
Tel :	(90-212) 671-0700 pbx
Fax :	(90-212) 671-0717
E-mail :	info@islamicpublishing.net
Web site :	http://www.islamicpublishing.net
Language :	English

ERKAM PUBLICATIONS

THE ISLAMIC APPROACH TO

Reason and Philosophy

OSMAN NÛRİ TOPBAŞ

ERKAM PUBLICATIONS

The Qur'an declares:

"Do they not meditate earnestly on the Qur'an, or are there locks on the hearts (that are particular to them, so that they are as if deaf and blind, and in- capable of understanding the truth)?" (47:24)

"Assuredly We have struck for humankind in this Qur'an all kinds of parables and comparisons, so that they may reflect and be mindful." (39:27)

"Assuredly We have set out in diverse ways for humankind in this Qur'an all kinds of parables and comparisons (to help them understand the truth); but human is, above all else, given to contention." (18:54)

❂

It is stated in a **Prophetic Tradition**:

"The wise person is the one who calls themselves to account (and refrains from doing evil deeds) and does noble deeds to benefit them after death; and the foolish person is the one who subdues themselves to their vain desires and merely hopes in Allah." (Tirmidhi, Qiyama, 25/2459)

❂

'Abd Allah ibn Mas'ud, may Allah be well pleased with him, says,

"Whoever seeks knowledge should reflect upon the meanings of the Qur'an and concentrate on its commentary and phonetics, for it contains the knowledge of former and future societies." (Haythami, VII, 165; Bayhaqi, Shu'ab, II, 331)

Sha'bi, may Allah have mercy on him, states,

"By Allah, if you were to follow the analogical deduction of a reason not resigned to the Divine revelation, then you would deem the prohibited permissible and the permissible prohibited." (Darimi, Muqaddima, 22/198)

Ibn Sirin, may Allah have mercy on him, says,

"Satan (Iblis) was the first to establish analogical reasoning. The sun was not worshipped nor was the moon except through analogical reasoning (i.e. based on arbitrary opinion independent of Revelation)." (Darimi, Muqaddima, 22/196)

Mawlana Jalal al-Din al-Rumi, may Allah have mercy on him, says,

"O brother! Find life with reflection... If your reflection is a rose (in line with the Qur'an and Sunna), you are in a garden of roses. If your reflection is a thorn (based on your carnal impulses), you are kindling for the bath stove."

"I am the servant of the Qur'an as long as I have life. I am the dust on the path of Muhammad, the Chosen one, upon him be peace and blessings. If anyone quotes anything except this from my sayings, I am quit of them and deplore their words..."

FOREWORD

Endless praise and thanks is due to our Lord Who created each of us out of nothing, made us the most honourable of creation, and favoured us with innumerable bounties – Islam, belief and the Qur'an first and foremost.

May endless peace and blessings be bestowed on all the Prophets who delivered humanity from the darkness of unbelief and ignorance and enabled them to attain eternal happiness, and especially upon our master Muhammad, the Pride of Humanity, may Allah bless him and grant him peace, and on all his Family and Companions.

Allah Almighty has created the human being in the most perfect form as a demonstration of His power and majesty. He has conferred upon them such lofty faculties as reason, heart, conviction and conscience in order for them to comprehend the truth of this world's being a realm of trial and examination and thus attain eternal happiness. Moreover, owing to these faculties being '**necessary**' but (on their own) **insufficient**' in thoroughly grasping truth and reality, He has perfected these bounties to humanity by sending them **Prophets** and **Scriptures**. What is more, out of His boundless mercy, He began sending Messengers with the very first human being so as not to deprive even a single individual of this blessing.

With respect to procedural laws pertaining to social life, God Almighty has communicated the Divine commands and prohibitions parallel to humanity's advancements over the centuries; in contrast, He has communicated the essentials of faith and belief perpetually along the same lines.

As an epilogue this grace, He has sent the **Qur'an** to humanity, with a scope and richness capable of meeting whatever needs may arise as long as the world stands. This grace is the most miraculous manifestation of Allah's mercy towards His servants which will continue until the Day of Judgement.

Allah Almighty has created only the jinn and human beings out of all created beings as subject to Divine trial, with a view to making known who would do good and who would commit evil. He has, therefore, equipped them with qualities and faculties open to both good and evil. He has created all other beings with the purpose of enabling these two classes of beings to attain the Divine truths and realise the necessary acts of worship.

This means to say that the reason for the creation of the universe is for human beings and the jinn to reach a perfected belief in the Creator's Existence, Oneness and Lordship and to glorify and exalt Him through worship.

The realisation of this purpose is contingent upon the virtues pertaining to humanity and the jinn being consolidated with the communication of the Prophets, and this is, at the same time, a Divine support granted to them.

Just as the eyes are in need of light in order to see, the mind and heart require the **Qur'an** and the **Sunna,** that is its practical application, in order to deepen in reflection and thus attain the Divine truths. For the human mind has been created to reach truth and goodness in the light of the Qur'an and Sunna. Were it not for the horizon of reflection paved by these two key sources, we could not have grasped a great many realities by means of reason alone and could not have expressed them. We could not have saved ourselves from perishing in the dark abysses into which many philosophers have fallen.

History is witness to the fact that neither those who have pledged philosophies offering peace and happiness only in the worldly sense have attained this peace, nor those following them, as there is no possibility for a philosopher, human beings in themselves, to know the truth of all creation better than its Creator. The Prophets who were favoured with Divine confirmation, however, and the scholars and Sufis following their example, have offered humanity the recipe for attaining happiness in this world and in the Hereafter and, as such, have continued living in hearts after their fleeting lives have come to an end.

Humanity has in no age or era been deprived of Divine communication and Prophetic instruction. They have continued their existence with the guidance of a reported one hundred and twenty four thousand Prophets and in approaching the end of time, were honoured with the final religion Islam, which responds to the needs of the time in the best possible way. Allah Almighty enabled Islam to reach perfection gradually through the Prophet's twenty-three year Prophethood and, as such, completed His favour upon His servants. From this point onwards, Allah Almighty declares that He approves only of Islam as a religion for His servants and that on no account will He accept any other from them.[1]

Islam possesses the most perfect worldview. In order for a system to be considered as having a perfected worldview, it needs to be able to provide answers to every conceivable question; moreover, these answers need to be consistent as a whole and

1.   See Ma'ida, 5:3; Al-'Imran, 3:19, 85.

display a logical progression and harmony. These characteristics, however, exist only within the **Islamic worldview**.

Islam has brought a worldview and rules for conduct encompassing all facets of life. It has regulated the relationship that human beings have with each other and, above all, with their Creator, with the most perfect principles, with all its details and without omitting any aspect of life. In this sense, it is like the user manual, as it were, for an electronic appliance.

Monotheistic religions corrupted by human intervention and especially worldviews invented by human beings themselves are replete with deficiency and contradiction.

Dear readers, today, we live in a world marked by attempts to imprison human comprehension within a materialist framework and polluted by earthly ambitions stemming from the relentless promptings of capitalism. Again, regretfully we witness human systems and schools of thought that are the product of reason suppressing religion and spirituality and attempting to exclude these from every field of life.

As a reaction to Judaism being subjected to alteration and human intervention and the contradiction-filled content of Christianity, the creed of which is determined by people convening at councils[2], there has been the attempt in the West to bring reason and the intellect to the fore and push religion into the background.

Naturally, thinking minds unable to find the answers they seek in a changed and distorted religion

---

2. The leading of the councils, which are an explicit example of exactly how a Divine religion is altered through human intervention, are the following:

In the **First Council of Nicaea** (Iznik) in AD 325, the status of Jesus as the 'son of God' was accepted, while the **First Council of Constantinople** (present-day Istanbul) in AD 381 settled the divinity of the Holy Spirit.

The **Council of Ephesus** (Efes) convened in Ephesus in AD 431 declared Mary the mother of Jesus "Theotokos", or "God-bearer". In addition, Jesus was declared both human and divine. At the **Council of Chalcedon**, held in AD 451, at Chalcedon (Kadıköy, Istanbul), repudiated the notion of a single nature in Christ, declared that he has two natures of divinity and manhood in one person (hypostasis) and denounced the Eastern Churches (Egyptian Coptics, Armenians, Assyrians and Abyssinian) that asserted a single nature, as deviant.

The **Second Council of Nicaea** convened in AD 787, declared that the use and veneration of religious images or icons was not a sin and lifted the ban on their use. Whereas close to 200 years prior, the question of whether or not the veneration of icons was a sin was debated and their use was sometimes banned by the Byzantine Emperor himself.

Whilst Eastern Orthodox Christians recognised the first seven councils, Catholic Christians accept the total twenty-one ecumenical councils until the last held in 1965. In this last ecumenical council, known as the **Second Vatican Council**, the Vatican called for dialogue with other denominations and religions.

have embarked on other quests. But, as most of them have been preconditioned over the centuries in a bigoted fashion against Islam, they have been deprived of the opportunity to realise where to find what they seek and to thus turn to Islam. For this reason, the number of those spurning the centuries-old dogmatisms to consider Islam, and in so doing, attaining the happiness they seek, is rather small. While this number has shown some increase with the advancing transport and communication technologies in recent years, it cannot be said to have reached a sufficient level. Therefore, it comes as no wonder that philosophy is in such demand in the West.

In addition, the West's important technological and economic advancements as a result of their dedication to research and their reaching a position of power and influence on the world platform has caused the erroneous assumption to spread rapidly and intensely in Muslim nations that reason needs to be put before religion in order to advance culturally and as a civilisation. Turning a blind eye to the fact that Muslims established the most magnificent civilisations throughout history when they were most faithfully devoted to Islam, there is an attempt to inculcate these distorted ideas across the Muslim world and in the minds of Muslims the world over.

It is crucial that Muslims and especially those preoccupied with the Islamic sciences be exceedingly careful and discerning in the face of this serious situation, for underlying an enthusiasm for Western philosophy is an inadequate knowledge and awareness of the brilliance of the **Islamic worldview**. This situation is identical to those filled with admiration for the flickering candlelight because they do not know the sun.

Moreover, where debates exist in our day about whether or not courses in philosophy should be included in the curricula of faculties of theology, we are faced with various questions concerning Islam's approach to '**reason and philosophy**' from students and those in our circles.

Faced with such a situation, we have deemed it necessary to present to our readers some of the matters that we have tried to express on different occasions, even if within a humble work such as this.

Works such as Kadir Mısıroğlu's *Islam Dünya Görüşü* (The Islamic Worldview), Necip Fazıl's *Batı Tefekkürü ve Islam Tasavvufu* (Western Thinking and Sufism), Imam Ghazali's *Munqiz min al-Dalal*, Imam Rabbani's *Maktubat* and various works by Bediüzzaman Said Nursi were referred to in the preparation of this booklet.

May Allah Almighty not deprive us of the spiritual blessing of His Word. May He keep us firm upon the luminous path of His Prophets, and the

scholars and saints who are their heirs. May He enable us to appreciate Islam the religion of truth, understand and practice it in the best way possible and thus include us all among those servants with whom He is pleased and who earn His favour.

Amin...[3]

Osman Nuri Topbaş
December 2013
Üsküdar, İstanbul

---

3.   I would like to express my gratitude to M. Akif Günay for his contribution to the preparation of this booklet and entreat Allah for all his efforts be a perpetual charity.

The Islamic Approach to Reason and Philosophy

Questions such as, 'What is the place of philosophy in Islam? To what point can reason, viewed by philosophy as the most important means to reaching truth, take a person? Does the scales of reason hold the power to weigh up all truths? How can progress be made after the point at which reason stalls?' continue to preoccupy human beings today as they have throughout history.

It must be stated at the outset that philosophy is based on human intellect. Islam, however, relies both upon the rational faculty (*'aql*), within its natural limits, and upon transmitted knowledge, or on the Qur'an and Sunna (*naql*). Even if there are similarities in respect of subject matter and objective, there are significant differences between a system of thought based on the Divinely revealed truths and a philosophy resting on a mind beset by human weakness and which is ultimately limited in capacity; these differences relate to method, means, thought and imagination.

Nevertheless, the expression, 'the Philosophy of Islam' implies the views of Muslim thinkers educated within Islamic thought or those who have placed greater emphasis on philosophy in their thought.[4] Sometimes, the expression is used to imply the transcendent truths of Islam. Otherwise it does not mean that Islam is conducive to philosophy.

For instance, Islam too is rationalist to a certain degree. Islam attaches great importance to reason, or the intellect to such an extent that it deems it as one of the two key conditions for being considered religiously and morally accountable (mukallaf) in the eyes of Allah. One of these conditions is reaching the age of puberty, while the other is being of sound mind and judgement. In other words, one's mental faculties must be developed to the level of being able to distinguish between the prohibited and permissible, sin and reward, right and wrong. For this reason, children and those afflicted with insanity are not considered accountable or responsible in Islam.

Placing such weight on the intellect, Islam encourages the believers to reflect upon the truths of

18

---

4. See Kadir Mısıroglu, Islam Dünya Görüşü Sebil Yayınevi, Istanbul 2008, 32-33.

life and universe and the wisdoms of the Divine Word at every opportunity. And this can only be realised with a **sound mind** not negatively preconditioned.

In addition, the limited nature of the intellect's capacity for comprehending truth and reality has been expressly declared in Islam, for Allah has not bestowed any unrestricted power to any of His creation.

The power that all created beings possess out of Divine grace are confined within certain limits. Human intellect can offer its owner only a limited opportunity to reach truth. The truths contained in life and the universe, however, do not pertain to the mind's sphere of authority and are themselves unbounded. This fact illustrates that human intellect is **necessary**, but **insufficient** in reaching a complete comprehension of truth and reality. It is for this reason that Muslim scholars have referred to reason as the **'imperfect intellect'** (*naqis al-'aql*) or the **'Partial Intellect'** (*'aql al-juz'i*).

It is again on this basis that belief is realised through **'avowal with the tongue and affirmation with the heart'** – not the mind. Even this Islamic principle demonstrates that that the desired objective cannot be reached with reason alone, but with an action of the heart – that is, through 'surrender' and 'presupposition' which begins at the point where reason runs short.

The truths to be obtained by means of the human intellect, no matter how high a level it achieves, amounts to a great 'nothing' before that which the Creator, Who possesses infinite knowledge, makes known.

As stated in a Qur'anic verse:

" ...Our Lord embraces all things within His Knowledge..." (7:89)

The knowledge of human beings, however, is oblivious even to what will befall it tomorrow.

From this standpoint, when reason is used in line with the commandments of the Lord Who created it, it would have realised its purpose in creation.

A Drop from the Ocean

No one can be as acquainted with the thought and feeling of someone who produces a masterpiece which helps shape that work, as the artist producing it. Similarly, it is impossible for a person, who is themselves created, to fully grasp the Divine truths hidden in all created things and events in their entirety, with their limited conception, as the knowledge of the created can never be equivalent to that of the Creator. Such comprehension is but a single drop before a vast ocean.

For this reason, human conception is unable to wholly comprehend God also, Who created the universe out of nothing. For the road of human knowledge is that of the five senses, the mind and the heart and the power of all these means of perception is limited. Complete comprehension of an exalted Being Who is Everlasting, Absolute and Eternal is not possible with means that are themselves limited in power.

Perception that can only be realised with limited means can itself only be limited. In other words, we can only take as much water from the ocean as our cup will allow.

The following Prophetic Tradition is a succinct expression of this truth:

"(During the journey in which Khidr showed Prophet Moses, upon them both be peace, various strange incidents with hidden wisdoms) a sparrow landed on the edge of the ship and dipped its beak into the sea. Drawing Prophet Moses' attention to this scene, Khidr said, "Your knowledge, my knowledge, and the knowledge of all creatures in respect of the knowledge of Allah is only like what this sparrow took with its beak." (Bukhari, Tafsir 18)

Stupefying Divine Mysteries

It is owing to the fact that a great many Divine truths cannot be comprehended with the mind that Islam commands 'belief in the Unseen'.

One of the strongest proofs of this reality is the historical contention and debate surrounding the **'nature of the spirit'**. As is known, philosophers have shown utmost effort throughout the centuries to get to the truth about the nature of the spirit. But ultimately deciding on the 'unknowability' of the spirit, they were forced to settle with purely accepting its existence on the basis of its behavioural manifestations.

Debate on this philosophical subject of inquiry continued over the centuries and the scholarly field of *'ilm al-nafs, ruhiyat*, or psychology in today's parlance, was established as a result. The subject of this discipline today is not an attempt to understand the nature of the spirit. After having adopted the existence of the spirit *a priori*, or through presupposition, it has been confined to examining the events proceeding from it and the relationships between these events and physical beings.

This state of affairs demonstrates that even philosophers have been forced to accept the limited nature of cognition. The philosopher in our day is no longer busy with study of the spirit's nature. The business of psychologists is comprised merely of investigating the causes and effects of spirit-related phenomena and their discipline has virtually become a 'laboratory science'. However, the Qur'an established this centuries ago, declaring that the nature of the spirit cannot be known and that very little information has been given to human beings concerning it.[5]

This means to say that the Qur'an is forever ahead, with human knowledge trailing behind and being constantly compelled to affirm it. Even this situation is a case in point demonstrating that the outcomes of all research activities undertaken in spite of the Qur'an end in disappointment and concession of weakness, and that there is no other option but to surrender to the Qur'anic truths.

In exactly the same way, obtaining truths relating to the Divine nature and essence is beyond the capac-

5.   See (17:85)

ity of the human mind. The outcome of these pursuits, too, amount to nothing other than a similar chagrin. This is why the Messenger of Allah, upon him be peace and blessings, said in this regard:

"Reflect on the signs of Allah, and do not reflect on His Essence, for you will never be able to give Him His due." (See, Daylami, II:56; Haythami, I:81; Bayhaqi, *Shu'ab*, I:136)

Ibn 'Arabi (d. 638/1240) stated, *"Know that whatever conception of Allah we form in our minds, He is other than it."*

This means that comprehending Allah Almighty, on the basis of the manifestations of His attributes, needs to culminate in a presupposition, in exactly the same way as in the matter of the spirit.

That is, Islam stipulates that we do not enter into dispute concerning such Divine mysteries and matters that are beyond human conception, and that we submit to the Divine decree. In fact, the word 'Islam' too is derived from the root *sa-li-ma*, and denotes submission and obedience to Allah, for belief necessitates the acceptance of truths that the scales of reason cannot measure and which transcend it.

As indicated in the Qur'anic chapter **Al-Kahf**, when **Prophet Moses**, peace be upon him, approached **Khidr**, peace be upon him, for the purpose of acquiring Divinely-inspired spiritual knowledge (*'ilm al-*

ladunni), and encountered certain mysterious manifestations beyond human conception, he was left in utter bewilderment. This was because it was Allah Almighty Who charged Khidr, peace be upon him, with such a task. As for Prophet Moses, peace be upon him, he was a great Prophet who brought the Divine law. However, Khidr's actions were those that were seemingly in contention with the Divine laws. Prophet Moses, peace be upon him, was faced with a formidable mystery. And when he could not discern the wisdom of the matter by reason, he objected.[67]

Khidr, however, had informed him at the very beginning of their acquaintance that he would not be able to show patience towards those things the inner reality of which he could not grasp. With these words, he indicated the inability of those remaining on the mental plane to grasp wisdom and the necessity of advancing on this path with the wings of surrender.

When Khidr, peace be upon him, explained the meaning behind several mystifying events, Prophet Moses, peace be upon him, realised firsthand that there are truths that reason is not capable of comprehending.

---

6.   See (18:66-82)

7.   *'Ilm al-ladunni*: A body of mysterious knowledge beyond human intellect and comprehension, which can only be acquired through the favour and will of Allah Almighty.

The following hadith concerning this narrative is related in Bukhari:

"May Allah have mercy on Moses. Would that he had been patient so that we would have been told more about them!" (Bukhari, Anbiya, 27; Ahmad ibn Hanbal, V, 118)

Thus, Islam entails belief, in full submission, to those truths of the unseen that no one other than God knows or which He reveals to those He wills and which cannot be evaluated with reason.

It is due to this that adequately fulfilling the search for truth that is a requirement of sound judgement is possible only with complete submission to the Divine Word.

Therefore, Islam's rationality is utterly unlike that of the **rationalist** philosophers who, in accepting the boundlessness of the power of reason in their search for truth, have virtually deified it. This is because Islam is a grounded system which evaluates the mind within its natural boundaries.

A Delicate Balance

Just as the eye's ability to see and the ear's ability to hear is limited, so too is the mind's cognitive capacity limited. There are countless beings which cannot be seen due to their being beyond the eye's limited vision. There are innumerable sounds which cannot be heard because of their remaining outside the ear's hearing level. Similarly, there are many truths that cannot be comprehended as they fall outside human comprehension. Reason is incapable of grasping these completely.

Great Muslim scholar **Ibn Khaldun**, considered to be the father of sociology and the philosophy of history, states:

"Human reason is a set of scales, a balance, whose capacity for measurement is exact but limited. But the intellect should not be used to weigh such matters as the Oneness of God, the Hereafter, the truths of Prophethood and realities beyond human comprehension. This is an effort in vain. One might compare this with a person

seeing a scale in which gold is being weighed and wanting to weigh mountains in it because it is so precise. **There is nothing to be said for the precision of the scales, but its capacity is limited.** *Similarly, the power of human reason, to know, reason and comprehend, also has a limit and cannot go beyond it.*"[8]

How beautifully the poet **Ziya Paşa** expresses this truth:

This small mind need not understand that lofty meaning,

For these scales cannot carry such a weight.

That is to say, the intellect has a certain limit at which it must stop, and beyond this is either insanity or misguidance. If one tried to operate a device manufactured to work with 220 volts of power with 2500 volts instead, that splendid device would immediately give way, regardless of how perfectly it was manufactured. The fact that certain philosophers who have taken the power of the intellect to be limitless ended their lives in mental institutions or by committing suicide is another expression of this reality.

---

8.   Ibn Khaldun, *Muqaddima*, 473.

Don't Seek Happiness in the Bazaar of Misery

Philosophers claiming to reach the truth without the guidance of Divine revelation have perpetually dragged the people they have managed to influence to misery instead of felicity, misguidance instead of truth.

In his work, *A'mâk-ı Hayâl* (The Depths of Imagination), **Shehbenderzade Ahmed Hilmi of Filibe** (Plovdiv) narrates, metaphorically, the path to turning this misery into bliss. In the following episode related in brief, the novel's protagonist **Raji**, who writhes in the spiritual crises of materialist philosophy and seeks peace and happiness, delves into the depths of imagination under the influence of the deep poetry recited by **Aynalı Baba**, in the accompaniment of a *saz* solo. He finds himself in an assembly where everyone, from the Prophets to the philosophers, eminent personalities to insignificant people, is present. A character representing all human beings, by the name of **Beşeriyet** ('Humanity'), crying his heart out, seeks a path to true happiness. Wailing in lamentation, he says, "Please tell me, take pity on me. I am both revolted by life and at the same time cannot do without it. Tell me, please! Tell me what is happiness?"

Some of the figures present stand up in response:

Confucius says, "Happiness is squeezing all flavours into a pot of rice."

"It is forever pondering greatness," Plato adds.

Aristotle exclaims, "Logic! This is happiness!"

Zoroaster defines it saying, "Happiness is not remaining in the dark."

"Happiness, you say?" Brahma remarks, "It is the exact opposite of what everyone thinks!"

Buddha cries out, "Happiness is one of the beautiful names of annihilation. It is Nirvana, O Humanity! Nirvana!"

Hearing these words, Humanity becomes completely confused.

"You haven't even been able to help yourselves and have spent your lives deprived of happiness. There is not single a trace of happiness in your words! You neither experienced happiness, nor allowed those following in your footsteps to do so."

The Prophets then described happiness. And finally, the master and seal of the Prophets, Prophet Muhammad, upon him be peace and blessings, addressed Humanity with the following words:

"O humanity! Happiness is accepting life and events as they are, it is being resigned to its burdens and exerting effort for its betterment."

Having found the answer he was looking for, Humanity stood up and said, "O Pride of Creation! O Mercy to All the Worlds! O illustrious Messenger! It is you, only you, who understands Humanity's troubles and has its cure!"[9]

Implied in these statements is the need to first accept the Divinely ordained circumstances (Absolute Decree or Destiny) without any objection, and as a result, not attempt to change them in vain.

This expresses the **'realism'** of the Islamic world-view. Because trying to change something that is based on Divine Determination is by no means possible, it amounts to nothing other than driving humanity to an extremely arduous but fruitless struggle.

9.   See, *Â'mâk-ı Hayâl*, Sebil Yayınevi, Istanbul 1993, 97-101; Akçağ Yayınları, Ankara 2004, 106-111.

Recipe for Peace: Resignation and Endeavour

This fleeting life, on the basis of its Divine wisdom of trial and examination in this world, is sometimes stage to the manifestations of wrath and sometimes to the manifestations of grace. The real attainment is to use our willpower in line with Allah's approval and to reap the fruits of all these Divine manifestations of wrath and grace. The Messenger of Allah, upon him be peace and blessings, has shed light on this truth as follows:

"What an extraordinary thing the business of the believer is! All of it is good for him. And that only applies to the believer. If good fortune is his lot, he is grateful and it is good for him. If something harmful happens to him, he is steadfast and that is good for him too." (Muslim, Zuhd, 64)

Consequently, the state of **'resignation'** that we need to display before the Divine decree is the first condition of human peace and happiness.

The second is exerting the effort to set right those things that can be rectified, despite life's burdens.

This demonstrates the existence of certain matters in life and events that are subject to human will and effort, or a limited freedom of action (*qadar al-muʿallaq*). A person's putting forth such an effort is, at the same time, a requirement of their being a **'possessor of freewill'**. Otherwise, abandoning oneself to the notion that nothing in life can be fixed drives humanity to despair and pessimism, and then to apathy and idleness. In other words, this spawns an apathy characterised by a failure to demonstrate freewill, through such statements as, "Oh well, this must be my destiny!"

And when the elevated virtues with which humanity is innately equipped are considered, it becomes clear that this amounts to nothing other than a fool's errand. In fact, what those in the West refer to as **'fatalism'** is in fact a demonstration of Divine destiny being thus misunderstood.

This is because in Islam, destiny has a **'suspended'** (*muʿallaq*) component, which is moulded in accordance with human freewill. This means that certain actions are created as a result of the servant's willing

34

them. Or else, the statement that is one of the essential principles of belief, "the good and evil of destiny are from God Most High," does not mean that everything has been unalterably determined by Allah. This statement instead expresses that Allah's will exists in every occurrence and that nothing that be realised without His knowledge and will.

If, in an action, Allah's will materialises first and a person's action follows, this is the 'Decree Determined' (qadar al-mutlaq). Examples of such include birth, death, race and lifespan. These circumstances can never be altered. However, a reward or punishment for the servant in the Hereafter is also not in question as a result. Such incidents only serve as a basis on which the measure of a servant's liability in the Hereafter will be determined.

In addition, Allah Almighty has also allowed human beings and the jinn, whom he has vested with a partial willpower, a certain degree of freedom of action. This situation implies that the servant's choice is actualised with Allah's permission and this is referred to as 'destiny suspended'. It is precisely due to the existence of such a scope of responsibility that the Messenger of Allah, upon him be peace and blessings, instructed human beings to put forth an endeavour to set right the wrongs in their lives.

This can be illustrated by means of the following example:

A father takes his child to a toyshop and says to her, "Choose whatever toy you like in the store, you are free to have whatever you wish." If, however, he informs her, in advance, of the beneficial and harmful ones of these toys out of his fatherly compassion, leaves her free to choose, and she chooses a harmful toy, he can leave her choice ineffectual by not paying for the item at the counter.

If he so chooses, he can also say as a requirement of his promise at the outset, "Have that toy and see for yourself, experience firsthand, the danger that I warned you about."

This world is like the toyshop in the example above and we resemble that child. The help that Allah Almighty has given us, by means of the Divinely-sent Prophets and Divine scriptures, is like that compassionate father's warning, *la tashbih wa la tamsil.*[10]

As He possesses universal Divine Will, Allah Almighty takes part in the servant's action with His attribute of 'Creator' and creates it. This is akin to that father's making the payment and actualising that

---

10. *La tashbih wa la tamsil*: Without drawing any comparison; without any resemblance to created things; without comparing Him.

child's wish. Our situation before events, the requirements of which we fulfil but which we are unable to
realise, is the same.

All these circumstances, as elucidated earlier, are
a result of humankind and the jinn being created for
the purpose of trial and examination in this worldly
arena.

What falls upon the servant in this regard is to
surrender their own will to the will of Allah and to
thus strive to reconcile their own wishes and inten-
tions with Divine approval and good pleasure, for as
is declared in a Qur'anic verse:

**"...It may well be that you dislike a thing but it
is good for you, and it may well be that you like a
thing but it is bad for you. Allah knows, and you do
not know."** (2:216)

As the Ant Sees It

There is another story in **Ahmed Hilmi of Filibe's** work *A'mâk-ı Hayâl*, concerning the inadequacy of the human mind. Again presented in summarised form, **Raji** goes to visit the Sufi **Aynalı Baba**[11] who he has not seen for quite some time.

After the exchange of short pleasantries, Aynalı Baba offers him some of the coffee to which he is accustomed and starts playing the reed flute. Whilst listening to this music, Raji once again delves into the depths of the realm of imagination and sees a dream. Essentially, life too is like a dream of sorts.

In his dream, he is supposedly an ant prince. Whilst being raised by special instructors in the palace, the teacher ant that provides lessons in geography obtains permission from the prince's father to take

---

11. Aynalı Baba is the Sufi that the young Raji, the novel's protagonist, meets frequently and during their meetings, delves into reverie, each representing an aspect of Sufi thought.

the prince out on a practical geography lesson. It is a pleasant, sunny day. While the teacher explains, "Here is such-and-such mountain, over there is such-and-such river," he is stopped by sudden thunder and a fierce flood begins sweeping the ants before him.

Possessing both an ant and a human perception, Raji sees, when looking at what is happening from a human perspective, that what the ants suspect to be thunder is actually the neighing sounds of two horses feeding nearby, while the heavy rain is their urinating at exactly the same moment.

The ants that are able to escape this catastrophe return to their school with their teacher. Everyone in the class provide rather scholarly and logical explanations as to the reasons behind this event on such a warm, sunny day, with their antly conception. However, none of these explanations have anything whatsoever to do with reality.

Raji knows that if he explains that he was able to see the event from a much broader perspective due his looking with human vision, nobody would believe him. For this reason, he listens patiently to these explanations that have nothing whatsoever to do with truth, and then suddenly imagines the state of the tired horses. He wakes from his dream in fits of laughter. He finds Baba laughing also, whilst mumbling a poem:

The sun burns, the world turns
They will all one day dwindle
O learned and talented one
Do you know the cause?[12]

As this story suggests, the human mind is no different to those ants with respect to comprehending the essence of the infinite truths in the universe. A human mind deprived of the guidance of Revelation and the realities acquired with the light of Prophethood is no different to the intellect of those ants, in terms of perceiving the manifestations of Divine power and majesty exhibited in the universe.

It ought to be stated here that another manifestation of Allah's mercy and grace upon humanity consists of dreams, for dreams are a guide for us to mentally attain the metaphysical realities of life. This is because many incidents that cannot possibly become realised in reality take place in dreams. This enables us to more easily grasp the veracity of Islam's declarations concerning the Hereafter.

All people purporting to show humanity the path to deliverance and acting as guides to them, save the Prophets and the righteous individuals following in the footsteps, and especially the philosophers presum-

---

12. See *Â'mâk-ı Hayâl*, Sebil Yayınevi, Istanbul 1993, 113-117; Akçağ Yayınları, Ankara 2004, 123-127.

ing to explain everything with their own intellect are forever inadequate – as in the example.

As the Prophets have relied on Divine revelation, they have come as guides to the truth confirming one another. The philosophers, however, been deprived of their Divine confirmation and have engaged in contemplation with their insufficient intellects, which have been subjected to the tyranny of their spiritually untrained egos. As a result, they have perpetually wasted their lives contradicting each other and refuting one another's system of thought.

French philosopher **Pascal** who, after spending a good part of his life struggling in philosophical whirlpools, came to understand the insufficiency of the mind and turned to a deep spiritual search, refers to the relativism of philosophy:

"There is almost nothing right or wrong which does not alter with a change in clime. A shift of three degrees in latitude is enough to overthrow jurisprudence. One's location on the meridian determines the truth, that or a change in territorial possession. Fundamental laws alter. What is right changes with the times. Strange justice that is bounded by a river or mountain! The truth on this side of the Pyrenees, error on the other."[13]

---

13.   Blaise Pascal, *Pensées* (1670).

What Use is Reason After One Has Missed the Boat?

It would be erroneous to suggest that the product of philosophical thought in its entirety is wrong, for philosophers are also able to reach certain truths to the extent of their observation of life and the universe, their reasoning and their contemplation.

For instance, the conclusion that mathematician and philosopher **Descartes** (1594-1650), who is considered to be the father of modern philosophy and rationalism, arrived at through his 'proof of existence' reasoning, is an expression of the necessity to accept the Divine revelation as the key source of truth and reality. In his *Metaphysical Meditations*, Descartes argues, "By 'God' I mean the very being the idea of whom is within me, that is, the possessor of all the perfections which I cannot grasp, but can somehow reach in my thought, who is subject to no defects whatsoever. It is clear enough from this that he cannot be a deceiver, since it is manifest by the natural light that all fraud and deception depend on some defect."[14] Accordingly, His knowledge too true and without defect. Because God is perfect, it is impossible for Him to be deceived. As He cannot be deceived, His knowledge is true. If He says that He has created the universe, this is also true and this must be so. It follows then that the source of true knowledge and certainty must be God, Who is "supremely good and the source of truth".

In reinforcing this same notion, Pascal asserts that there is a voice coming from within the core of our being which makes known to us our immortality, and this is the voice of Divine guidance becoming manifest within us.

While reaching the conclusion that belief in God's existence is a rational necessity, Descartes, Spinoza, Pascal, Kant and similar philosophers recognised the principles of a religion corrupted at the hand of human beings and due to their failure to adequately know Islam – a direct result of the 'negative preconditioning' mentioned earlier – they were unable to develop this notion. In fact, there is no surviving record or evidence of such philosophers with a

---

14.   René Descartes, *Descartes: Meditations on First Philosophy: With Selections from the Objections and Replies*, Cambridge University Press, 1996, 35.

reverence for religion being honoured with belief in God's Oneness and Unity, the first and fundamental condition of attaining happiness in this world and in the Hereafter. In the words of renowned Turkish poet **Necip Fazıl**, they resemble those, "Who have missed the last ferry after having reached the threshold of the wharf of Islam because of their failure to take a single further step."[15]

What good is an intellect and philosophy that does not allow one to take the step over the threshold of eternal deliverance after having come all the way to that threshold?

Necip Fazıl's words are again noteworthy:

"Philosophy, the institution established by the intellect to demonstrate its own sovereignty... And the institution of redressing the wrong, not finding the right... Every school in philosophy speaks the truth while showing the error of the other."[16]

Consequently, with the views of the religious philosophers being an antidote for the denial poison of the atheist and materialist philosophers and invalidating them, they are not entirely ineffectual. Indeed, it is well known that the philosophers opposed to religion who

---

15. Necip Fazıl Kısakürek, *Batı Tefekkürü ve Islam Tasavvufu (Western Thought and Sufism)*, Büyük Doğu Yayınları, Istanbul 2012, 51.

16. *Batı Tefekkürü ve Islam Tasavvufu*, 14.

closed their minds and hearts eternally to the proofs put forth by the Qur'anic verses and Prophetic Traditions as a result of their negative preconditioning, were able to be silenced again with proofs coming from within philosophy.

In fact, indicating that one need not reject the products of philosophical thought that are congruous with the Qur'an and that what is necessary at this point is to differentiate between truth and falsehood, **Said Nursi** says:

"...The philosophy the Risale-i Nur strikes at fiercely and attacks is not absolute, but the harmful sort. For the philosophy and wisdom that serve the life of human society, and morality and human attainments, and industry and progress, are reconciled with the Qur'an. Indeed, such philosophy serves the Qur'an's wisdom and does not oppose it. This sort the Risale-i Nur does not bother with.

As for the other sort, since it both leads to misguidance, atheism, and the swamp of nature, and is the cause of vice and dissipation, heedlessness and misguidance; and since with its spellbinding wonders it opposes the Qur'an's miraculous truths; the Risale-i Nur attacks and deals slaps at it with the powerful proofs in the comparisons contained in most of its parts. It does not attack beneficial, rightly-guided philosophy."[17]

"The soulless, dim truths of philosophy cannot clash with the brilliant, living truths of the Qur'an."[18]

From another standpoint, the human intellect according to the *Ahl al-Sunna* majority, can only grasp God's existence. It is deemed to be inadequate for anything beyond this, or in grasping His essential (*dhati*) and affirmatory (*thubuti*) Divine attributes, believing in His transcendence – His being above having any imperfections or deficiencies and His possessing all the attributes of perfection and His being the sole One worthy of worship – and in finding the truths He revealed to humanity.

Just as we are able to comprehend certain things with our mind that we cannot perceive with our sensory organs, we can only perceive certain things that the mind cannot comprehend, via Prophetic conveyance.

By way of example, **Imam Rabbani** states:

"The mind accepts the need for thankfulness to the provider of the bounty, but only the Prophets can communicate how this thankfulness is to be realised...

17. See, Said Nursi, *The Staff of Moses*, Sözler Publications, Istanbul 2002, 2.

18. Said Nursi, *The Words*, Sözler Publications, Istanbul 1992, 361.

Expressions of reverence and gratitude not learned from Allah are not admissible before Him... More often than not, a person makes utterances for the purpose of exalting Allah; however, far from exalting Him, these words, in reality, serve to do the opposite. The only path to learning how we are to be thankful to Allah is Revelation."[19]

Consequently, the intellect is in absolute need of the assistance of Revelation. Without this Divine aid, the comprehension of humanity would not be able to reach perfection and it could not free itself from being dragged into contradiction.

As a result, religion-denying atheists and materialist philosophers aside, the views of philosophers attaching importance to religion must also be weighed against Islamic truths and rights separated from wrongs.

In this respect, a philosophy not nourished from the 'religion of truth' cannot acquaint the human being with truth and reality. Only the religion of truth can put forth absolute and eternal beliefs that are not relative and ephemeral, as the Prophets do not speak from their own whims and vain desires. They convey the **commandments of Allah Almighty**. As for the philosophers, they say, **"This is how it is in my opinion,"** and make subjective and relative judgements.

---

19.   *Maktubat*, v. III, Twenty Third Letter.

The Need for a Tangible Measure

In point of fact, no society throughout the history of humanity can be shown to have implemented the views of any particular philosopher and to have thus attained peace and happiness. The ideas they propounded remained nothing other than dry theories impossible to be put into practice and, for the most part, were doomed to imprisonment in books upon dusty shelves. Others, which were implemented to a certain extent, were to no avail other than dousing the earth with blood and tears and were soon after consigned to the scrapheap of history.

For instance, despite **Aristotle**'s having formed the basis of a number laws and principles of moral philosophy, even a single person cannot be shown who has attained happiness through belief in his philosophy and putting it into practice.

Plato's *Republic* utopia has not gone beyond an imaginary conception of state.

Again, the *al-Madinat al-Fadila*, which presents the 'virtuous city and ideal society' envisioned by *Al-Farabi* who stressed philosophy despite being raised in the Muslim world, has found no opportunity of application. This is because just as these are not truths that were penned as a result of experience, they did not possess the characteristics allowing them to be lived after having been written.

Nietzsche, the most salient example of this in the West, envisioned a **'superhuman'**, or ideal human being. However, the virtues he portrayed for such a person remained a simple theory bereft of exemplars, or models that were worthy of emulation, as well as the possibility of practical application.

Whereas Islam is an ideal system possessing such effective criteria as the exemplary lives of the Prophets in addition to the tangible standards of perfected behaviour and conduct. Such qualifications as truth and falsehood, right and wrong, beautiful and repugnant are each as good as labels. You can use these in relation to whatever attitude you wish. However, when these labels are not consolidated with practical, actual examples, the possibility of their being used for erroneous attitudes will forever remain.

However, by elevating His Messenger, upon him be peace and blessings, from society's most helpless status of orphan, to the rank of head of state and to Prophethood, Allah Almighty rendered each and every one of the perfect actions emanating from him an effective criterion, or benchmark of behaviour, as well as a life's motto.

Allah Almighty revealed the Qur'an not in an instant or in a short period of time, but gradually, over the course of the Prophet's twenty-three years of Messengership. Each verse of Divine Ordinance was first expounded and set forth by Allah's Messenger, the Fine Exemplar, in living form.

As with the Qur'an, these perfect examples from the conduct of Allah's Messenger, upon him be peace and blessings, were preserved with respect to their each being a tangible norm. And these have been bestowed upon his community as practical examples for all modes of conduct and behaviour. As Nietzsche did not possess such effective criteria, his 'superhuman' is doomed to remain a utopian theory. No system of ethics that is the product of human reason possesses the perfection in operational criteria that Islam possesses.

During every era in which the truths exhorted by the Prophets and the saintly scholars and gnostics following in their footsteps were taken as an example, societies attained peace and happiness, for Allah Almighty presents His Messenger, upon him be peace and blessings, as the best exemplar of perfection of all human behaviour. As declared in a Qur'anic verse:

"Assuredly you have in Allah's Messenger an excellent example to follow for whoever looks forward to Allah and the Last Day, and remembers and mentions Allah much." (33:21)

Human beings who stooped to the lowest level with respect to their humanity, through their ignorance and the intensity of their persecution, rose to the summit in humanity, virtue, morality, mercy, compassion, truth and justice by receiving a share in the exemplary manner and behaviour of Allah's Messenger, as well as in his communication of the message and guidance.

The words of **Qarafi** (d. 684), one of the most important figures of Islamic law, constitute a concrete example of this fact:

"If Allah's Messenger, upon him be peace and blessings, had no other miracle, nothing more than the Companions that he cultivated would stand as sufficient proof of his Prophethood."

The members of that society, rescued from the darkness of associating partners with Allah and the barbarity of the Age of Ignorance through the Prophetic training with which they were honoured, each became stars shining in the firmament of human virtue. For the generations of believers following them, they built a magnificent Islamic civilisation which humanity still beholds with envy.

On the basis of the Prophet's success in his mission, French historian and thinker Lamartine expresses what great genius Allah's Messenger, upon him be peace and blessings, possesses, as follows:

"If greatness of purpose, smallness of means, and astonishing results are the three criteria of a human genius, who could dare compare any great man in history with Muhammad?

The most famous men created arms, laws, and empires only. They founded, if anything at all, no more than material powers which often crumbled away before their eyes.

This man moved not only armies, legislations, empires, peoples, dynasties, but millions of men in one-third of the then inhabited world."[20]

Again, the English writer **Thomas Carlyle** said:

"No emperor with his tiaras was obeyed as this man in a cloak of his own clouting."[21]

---

20. Alphonse de Lamartine, *Histoire de la Turquie.*
21. Thomas Carlyle, *The Best Known Works of Thomas Carlyle: Including Sartor Resartus, Heroes and Hero Worship and Characteristics,* Wildside Press LLC, 2010, 202.

This is because Allah's Messenger, the Pride of Creation, did not speak of his own vain desire or whim, but served as humankind's interpreter to the Divine Revelation. For this, he was favoured with Divine support.

One of the eras, after the Age of Happiness, in which Islam was practised in the most radiant manner was undoubtedly during the **Ottoman state**. The Ottomans followed in the Prophet's footsteps with a great faithfulness, sincerity and love and attained the level of a magnificent civilisation.

Indeed, the inspiration for Western utopian writer and Italian philosopher **Tommaso Campanella**'s work *The City of the Sun*, was the civilisational splendour of the Ottoman state. This case constitutes one of the innumerable demonstrations of the fact that humanity can only attain peace and tranquillity through Islam, the religion of life, not through manmade philosophies of life that are impossible to implement in practice.

Had the Intellect Been Enough

Allah Almighty certainly knows His servants, Who He created out of nothing, much better than they know themselves. Hence, in order to redress the weakness and inadequacy of human reason in reaching the truth, He sent throughout human history, according to narration, 124,000 Prophets and made His great support felt by means of the Divine books He revealed to human beings to enable them to reach the truth. Even this situation is enough to show that the intellect, or human reason, is not sufficient in reaching truth, goodness and reality. Had the intellect been a sufficient means in this respect, Allah Almighty would not have sent all these Prophets and Books to humanity.

From another perspective, whatever their living conditions, all humanity experiences a shared shudder before the reality of **death**. The eventual fading of the winding paths of life in the horizon of death causes hearts profound anguish.

Attempts have been made in every age to silence, suppress or imprison to one's subconscious via various falsehoods, the unknowns relating to **death** and the **afterlife** – which have settled in minds like a poisonous snake and have made human beings anxious each time it stirred. This conundrum concerning the future, which cannot possibly be solved with the human mind, can only be resolved by the voice of revelation.

The sole Divine Book which makes the unknowns in this fleeting journey of life known, which unravels its mysteries, illuminates its darkness and encompasses, in every way, the most satisfactory proofs for the mind and heart, is the **Qur'an**.

Allah Almighty invites us, in a great many verses of the Qur'an, to reflect upon the wisdom of the creation of human beings, the spectacular order in the universe and the Qur'an being a miracle of speech and expression. Those wanting to live their lives in a manner befitting their dignity as human beings are obliged to enter this Qur'anic-oriented world of reflection.

Like the stupendous majesty acquired by the minuscule sycamore seed by means of a fertile soil and its turning into a huge tree, the spiritual perception and truths that can be reached through our contemplation, imagination and emotion, are magnificent and infinite. In this respect, were it not for the

Qur'an's inexhaustible spiritual effusion and exalted guidance, our contemplation and sensibility would have remained like a dry seed deprived of a productive earth.

Therefore, there cannot be a greater bounty for us as human beings than to comprehend the loftiness and grandeur of a Divine favour realised by means of the Qur'an.

Indeed, societies cannot attain soundness with the ideas of pedants stooped over the books of philosophy, which sit upon the dusty shelves of libraries. That which is to carry humanity to true happiness and salvation is the communication, counsel and guidance of the believers who have been shaped by the **Qur'an** and the culture of its 'living annotation' that is the **Prophetic Practice** and who have reached perfection with Divine wisdom and reality.

A reason not trained under the guidance of Divine declaration resembles a rampant horse. Just as it is not possible to reach one's goal with it, eventual ruin is inevitable. This being so, in the same way that one must rein back a wild horse and train it in order to benefit from its energy in the best possible way, it is essential that the intellect is placed under the spiritual tutelage of **Revelation,** and the **Sunna** that constitutes its interpretation, and is transformed into **sound judgement**.

Philosophical schools claim to understand truth without the communication and guidance of the Prophets who were favoured with Divine confirmation and support. The greatest truths, however, cannot be learned without the mediation of the exceptional servants to whom Allah conferred the distinction of Prophethood.

Mawlana Jalal al-Din al-Rumi depicts this point in the following way:

"Even a child's reason says, 'Busy yourself with books.' But it is not possible for a child to learn anything from a book on their own.

Like so, the patient's reason brings them to a physician, but their reason cannot be a cure for them.

If every blabbermouth was to find a way to Allah's grace and favour, would Allah Almighty have sent all these Prophets?"

The Prophets are the greatest grace of Allah upon all humanity. Human beings could not acquire even a tiny amount of the magnificent knowledge that the Prophets imparted, without expecting anything in return, concerning the Divine essence and attributes, with thousands of years of philosophical thought, inquiry, investigation, observation and self-purification.

Imam Rabbani says in this regard:

"The Prophets are a mercy to the worlds. By means of these lofty individuals, Allah Almighty revealed His Own Essence and Attributes to such possessors of partial intellect ('aql al-juz'i) as human beings, and made known the supremacy pertaining to His Essence and Attributes in proportion to their comprehension. Again through the Prophets, He informed humanity of those things with which He is pleased and those things of which He disapproves, and allowed them the opportunity to distinguish their worldly and otherworldly interests from their harms. Without the Prophets, human intellect could not have (adequately) perceived Allah's existence, nor grasped His exaltedness."[22]

Seeing that as truths will come to an end at the point where the power and authority of the human intellect runs short, the inclination to continue on towards endlessness after this point, and thus reach truth cannot be averted. Because this is an instinctive, natural need. As a result, this aspect of truth and reality has not been neglected in the religion, or in non-religious thought. It is well known that philosophical thought pertaining to metaphysical matters constitutes an enormous corpus.

22.   *Maktubat*, v. III, Twenty Third Letter.

As indicated earlier, while the Prophets, who benefited from the Divine wellspring, perpetually confirmed one another throughout history, the philosophers who took human reason as a basis could not escape contradiction, and each emergent philosopher began their task with rejection and criticism of those who came before. Even if ego and the primacy of worldly claims have a great role to play in this, the real reason is the intellect's inability to remain free of contradiction.

Indeed, the information put forth by human intellect can never be completely purified of the threat of doubt, hesitation, error, deficiency, forgetfulness and delusion. This is because the intellect remains under the influence of opinion, stereotyped notions and external positive and negative suggestions. Whether this influence is to a small or large degree, it is always a given. It cannot be completely free of such weaknesses as greed, anger and vain desire, and from such flaws as absentmindedness and error. A great many judgements that it makes emerges after having been imbued and distorted with the hue of these external colours. In other words, human intellect is not an infallible source in the acquisition of information.

If Great Minds Think Alike

There is a famous story stemming from Ancient Greece demonstrating the weakness of the intellect. A young man by the name of Euathlus, studied law under the tutelage of the famous sophist (systematic philosopher of rhetoric and dialectic) **Protagoras**. Protagoras, recognising his talent, accepts Euathlus as his student on the condition that Euathlus pay him half of the money up front and the other half after he wins his first court case. This implied that, in the event of the student's having won his first case, the instruction was of a very high standard and the teacher qualified for the second instalment.

But Euathlus successfully finished his course of study, but asked his teacher to waive the second instalment. Protagoras then decided to sue Euathlus for the amount owed.

When they appeared before the judges, Protagoras offered the following argument:

"If Euathlus loses this case, then he must pay (by the judgment of the court). If Euathlus wins this case, then he must pay (by the terms of the contract). He must either win or lose this case. Therefore Euathlus must pay me."

But Euathlus, who had learned well the art of rhetoric, countered:

"Not so! If I win the case, then by the court's decision I would not have to pay Protagoras. If, on the other hand, Protagoras wins, then I would still not have won a case and would therefore not be obliged to pay (as per the contract). I must either win or lose the case. Therefore, I do not have to pay Protagoras."[23]

As is evident, the claims of both are rather rational and logical. This means that reason and logic, as demonstrated in the example, can from time to time imprison itself within its self-established walls and find itself in an impasse. Just like the self-contradiction inherent in putting up a sign on a wall which reads, "Putting up signs not permitted!"

Can it at all be possible for an intellect weak and brought to a deadlock even in the face of such examples of human dilemma, to grasp the eternal Divine truths with all their facets? If this is the case for

23.   See *Islam Dünya Görüşü*, 267-268; *Batı Tefekkürü ve Islam Tasavvufu*, 22-23.

a human being in a worldly matter, then what would their predicament be in the countless otherworldly, celestial, spiritual and religious matters which cannot be known and discovered without the help of Divine revelation? Complete weakness, incapacity and deficiency...

Hence, the intellect's freedom from such impasses is connected to its being trained with Divine revelation and its coming to a realisation of the need for a heartfelt submission to those truths which exceed its boundaries.

A Symbol of Inconsistency: Positivism

The views of all materialist philosophies which reject the transcendent truths of religion hinge on **positivism**. Positivist philosophy accepts only the five senses as sources of knowledge in reaching truth.

According to this philosophy, there is no truth to anything that cannot be perceived through the sensory organs in a laboratory. Consequently, truth merely possesses qualities that can be proven via laboratory experiments and controlled with the five senses. However, as Islam commands belief in the 'Unseen', which the five senses are incapable of perceiving, its greatest adversaries are the positivist philosophies.

Positivism is based on the two basic principles, which contrast sharply with positivism itself. The first of these is the principle of **universality**, while the other is the principle of **necessity**.

The principle of universality is the following:

63

The quality ascribed to a single entity is consistent throughout the universe. For example, if one were to heat pure water in a laboratory, under normal conditions of pressure, that water would evaporate when it reached a certain temperature. A scientist established the unit by which the boiling point of water would be measured by expressing this boiling point with the numerical value of 100. It was thus claimed that all water boils at the same temperature. Other realities of the physical world are realised according to the positivist understanding in this way.

However, only a limited number of water samples can be examined and tested in a laboratory, even if these numbered in the thousands. While there is left remaining infinite amounts of water that has not been tested, the positivist asserts, "All water reaches boiling point at 100 degrees Celsius." But this is for them a contradiction, as they cannot accept the accuracy of a claim that has not been tested in the laboratory. Despite this, when asked, "How can you make such a claim without first verifying all kinds of water through scientific experiment?" they respond, "As it is impossible to test all kinds of water, we can generalise our findings after having tested a certain number of water samples and observed them to conform to the same fact."

The acceptance of religious truths is also thus. When observant individuals observe the rationality in the religious commandments, which are able to be perceived with the five senses, and see its continuation over time, they accept and affirm the continuance of this rationality in matters that they cannot comprehend.

For instance, a person who reflects upon the innumerable episodes of God's creating and sustaining living beings with His infinite power can readily comprehend precisely how He is capable of reviving all living beings after their death. Likewise, a person observing that Allah Almighty has not neglected a single creature and that He grants each of them their sustenance comes to understand that He is capable of calling all His servants to account on the Day of Rising. Such a person reaches an acceptance and affirmation in truths that they cannot observe on the basis of such realities that can be observed in this way.

Despite the fact that positivists accept this circumstance for themselves, they deem this irrational for religious individuals and reject all metaphysical truths. They thus contradict themselves.

This contradiction is essentially the common paradox of all philosophical schools opposed to God's Unity and Oneness. **Imam Rabbani** refers to the inherent inconsistency of the philosophers opposing the Divine truths:

"How strange it is that these individuals spend a lifetime learning the science of logic which prevents the human mind from making errors in reasoning, and learn its minutest details. But when it comes to such important matters as the Divine essence, attributes and acts of God, they lose themselves, forget the science of logic and begin speaking nonsense. Their situation resembles that of a person who devotes many years to preparing weapons for warfare and, when the time comes, loses themselves and forgets how to use the weapons."[24]

The second underlying principle of positivist thought is **necessity**. While positivists cannot explain the inherent characteristics of things and the differences between them by means of scientific experiment, they refer to these as **necessities** and accept them.

Whereas according to positivists, because every hypothesis must be verified scientifically, their embracing the inherent characteristics of living beings on the basis of presupposition, constitutes for them a blatant contradiction.[25]

For example, positivists content themselves with merely identifying the reaction differences that various physical entities exhibit in evaporation, specific

---

24. *Maktubat*, v. III, Twenty Third Letter.
25. See *Islam Dünya Görüşü*, 46, 269.

weight or external influences, and do not investigate their causes. This is because the purpose of creation is beyond their area of interest. They do not reflect upon such matters. Islam, however, sets forth these characteristics via the wisdom of 'Divine determination and regulation', in a manner befitting the purpose for the existence of all created beings.

The Qur'an exhorts all believers reading the 'book of the universe', **"Read in and with the Name of your Lord, who has created."**(96:1) This means to say, it commands observation of the Divine names, attributes and manifestations of majesty exhibited in the universe and enjoins moving from the art to the artist and from creation to the Creator, intellectually and at heart. It exhorts human beings to look at the universe not for the universe itself, but for the sake of its Creator.

Materialist philosophy, however, looks at created beings for their own sake. In other words, it views creatures – by ruling out their Creator – with a materialist eye. It does not wish to see the artist, despite seeing the art, and shuns looking at the handiwork and contemplating the maker. While demonstrating the infecundity and deficiency of materialist philosophy's view of the universe, this is a vivid illustration of the expansiveness, depth and perfection of Islam's outlook.

Moreover, according to Islam, the sole absolute and necessarily existent being is Allah Almighty. All beings other than Allah are indebted to Him for their existence. Thus, the **human being** is not an absolute, but a contingent being.

Philosophies claiming to reach truth without reliance on religion hold the human being at the centre and view them as the absolute reality, while setting out to evaluate other creatures in relation to and dependent on them. Spurring on the Pharaoh of egocentrism and arrogance of Nimrod, as to claim, "The world revolves around me," they exemplify, as it were, the unfortunate souls decried in the Qur'anic verse, "Do you ever consider him who has taken his lusts and fancies for his deity?"(45:23) Drawing a veil over such inborn deficiencies as error, forgetfulness, weakness, incapacity, need and transience, they strive to make the human being forget their status as 'servant'. Displaying the simplicity of ascribing the life and worldly bounties bestowed by Allah Almighty to nature and coincidence, they attempt to shut the door to servitude and gratitude to Him. It is well known that all these constitute the greatest objective of Satan, a manifest enemy of humankind.

A branch of positivist philosophy, which forms the essence of all anti-religionist thought, has been formed in such a manner as to encompass all spheres of life. For instance, with communism in economic life and Freudianism in sexuality, various anti-Islamic theories have been propounded and put into practice. All of these are repudiated due to their being based on positivist thought – with positivist thought being deficient with respect to attaining truth and reality – and the opposition of these to Islam constitutes for them a contradiction and illogicality.

Human Reason: A Double-Edged Sword

"Those who suppose the human intellect to possess a limitless power are compelled to accept that people possessing intellect should not commit any crime. After all, if human intellect is capable of reaching truth and reality, then why should an intelligent person commit an offence? Why should they be the perpetrator of an illegal act? While all man-made systems punish the offender, they do so in acknowledgement of their soundness of mind. In the event that they are convinced of the offender's mental faculties being impaired during the actual committing of the crime, they do not punish the offender.

This means that the logical premise for punishment is to accept that the perpetrator is of sound mind. In this case, believing in the intellect as a sufficient means to reach truth while at the same time punishing it for its felony is an inherent contradiction. Due to the fact that Islam, however, deems the intellect necessary but insufficient, it is far from such a contradiction."[26]

Human reason is like a doubled-edged sword. It can be a means to good as well as to evil. Murder can be committed with it, as can good works. A servant cannot reach the highest possible spiritual level without the aid of reason; however, that which reduces a person to the position of **"even more astray [than animals] (from the right way and in need of being led)"**[27] is more often than not their intellect.

---

26. See *Islam Dünya Görüşü*, 36.
27. See (7:179; 25:44).

The Abdication of Reason

Philosophers have identified certain truths with their reason and have developed systems of thought upon these. However, these systems have done more harm than good. Moreover, another matter in which they have been mistaken is their presuming to explain the human reality on the basis of a single tendency. It is their seeing a sole truth, which they have ascertained concerning the human reality, as the only inclination to which all other vital inclinations are connected, by giving it a higher level than it deserves or by broadening its scope. These are 'monist' theories.

For instance, the Jewish **Sigmund Freud** (d. 1939) urged a simple – as good as animalistic – and principally base worldview for human beings with the theory he put forward. With the sleight of oversimplifying countless and elaborate truths, he led the human being to a moral dissipation and indignity. Bringing the human sexual drive to the fore, he explained all life activities in their entirety by means of this, and presented the 'libido'[28] as the key cause of all events.

Indeed, this inclination is one that is inborn and it has a certain level of influence on behaviour. But Freud's fallacy, is his extending this inclination to every domain of human life and his seeing this as the chief motive of all behaviour. This state is no different to looking at a very small object with a lens and magnifying it to such an extent that one is unable to see anything else.

This precisely is one of the main differences between Islam's rationality and the rationalism of Western philosophy. Western rationalism is one which oversimplifies grand and multifaceted truths, seeks to present a single part as the whole and which therefore cannot be secure against error and contradiction.

The rationality of Islam, however, is a rationality which sees the part within the whole, looks at the detail from the whole and which, as such, attaches as much value on that detail as it deserves and evaluates it alongside all the other parts. It is unifying, is based on oneness and integrity and forever remains faithful to this principle.

---

28. Libido: In Freudian doctrine, the force or psychic energy behind the sexual urge.

In fact, Islam too accepts sexual inclination as a reality. It does not deny, but regulates this inclination granted by Allah for the continuation of the human race. By means of its regulations concerning marriage, it places it within a framework of legitimacy. Whilst deeming it lawful and acceptable within this framework, it prohibits – on the basis of myriad purposes and wisdoms – that which remains outside the sphere of the prescribed.

In the same way, due to the fact that **Karl Marx**, **Darwin** and like materialists have been deprived of the guidance of a Divine revelation protected against distortion, they have viewed the human being as merely a biological being and have thus denied their inner world, ultimately giving rise to the spiritual and social squalor of millions of people. The utopia of communism, throughout the entire twentieth century that was marked by the attempt to realise it in practice, was to no avail other than to darken the life of the people living under its territory or sphere of influence in this world and the Hereafter.

Bringing economics to the fore, **Karl Marx** presumed to explain life and all events through this means. In other words, he took a single part and ignored all the others. Thus, when the intellect is deprived of the guidance of Divine revelation, it becomes imbalanced. And what happens as a result? The **liberalists** who see life as made up of economics do not give weight to the question of whether one's earnings are lawful or not, **capitalists** turn the human being into merely a cogwheel facilitating the operation of the economy wheel, and **communists** and **socialists** spend a lifetime squabbling over the owner of property.

These and similar man-made systems have no spiritual side. They have neither compassion, nor justice tempered by mercy, nor understanding...

Islam, however, accepts material necessity and need as one of a great many realities and has placed as much importance on it as it deserves. It has regulated this reality also, in the light of revelation, in a manner consonant with the peace and happiness of human beings, indicating the paths of a lawful and legitimate livelihood.

Moreover, Islam announces that dominion belongs neither to the individual, nor to society, but only to Allah Himself. It reveals that the Muslim serves but the role of temporary treasurer over property, in the name of the Creator. Declaring that the world will remain still in the world, it declares that the human being will shape their eternal life in the Hereafter with what they do in this worldly arena of examination. It has rendered the individual responsible for society.

Through such Prophetic statements as, *"One who sleeps on a full stomach while his neighbour is hungry*

is not a (perfected) believer," [29] and "Those who are not grieved by the plight of the believers are not of us," [30] it has assigned the Muslims to each other's care and, as such, has realised social justice and cooperation in the best possible way. Such periods have been witnessed during Islam's history, as during the caliphate of 'Umar ibn 'Abd al-'Aziz, that it was not possible to find needy people to whom the alms-tax could be given.

Again as a result of this Islamic sensibility, the Ottomans left no societal wound untreated with its 26 thousand-odd charitable trusts that functioned as its institution of mercy. In this way, the emergence of feelings of animosity, envy and hostility in society's impoverished towards the rich was prevented and social peace and tranquillity ensured.

Islam has regulated economics also, like all realities which hold a place in human life, with a perfection conducive to the happiness of the individual and society in this world and in the world to come.

Consequently, the realities which can be deemed 'rational' for a Muslim are those realities congruent with the Divine commandments and which offer a depth and scope that take this world and the Hereafter into constant consideration.

29.   Hakim, II, 15.
30.   Hakim, IV, 352; Haythami, I, 87.

From this perspective, a Muslim is always mindful of their Creator, Who created all beings from nothing and gave life to them, the Transcendent Being of a perfection that is beyond comprehension. They find peace inwardly with the hope of union with Him in the Hereafter. There is no peace and reassurance that philosophies that are the product of human intellect can offer in this regard.

For this reason, Islam does not find reasonable many deeds and ideas that Western rationalism deems rational and logical. For instance, it does not regard the intellect of those who misuse it and drift into unbelief, or those who make light of the religious injunctions, or those who make allowances for any act of immorality, as sound. This is because the intellect is intellect so long as it surrenders to absolute truth.

The famous poet **Fuzuli** alludes to the weakness of an intellect, which fails to submit to the Divine truths and goes its own way, in the following couplet:

From my mind I seek guidance,

But it offers only misguidance.

In other words, he says, "I want for my mind to guide me to truth, while it, on the contrary, leads me to deviation and falsehood."

Furthermore, it is not only the intellect that determines a person's bearing and behaviour. A person makes decisions in their life more on the basis of emotion than on reason. As a consequence, it is crucial that not only the intellect as the centre of thought is trained and cultivated under the guidance of the Divine truths in reaching truth and goodness, but the heart as the centre of emotion, is trained and cultivated also. This, in turn, necessitates a spiritual training that ensures purification of the mind and heart and feeling, thought and behaviour being steered towards the Divine truths.

Otherwise, a person cannot be freed from the unforeseen perils into which mental faculties and emotional inclinations will drag them and waste their life in the heedlessness of supposing their wretchedness to be prosperity. Such a person will still see himself or herself to be faultless despite being steeped in error and wrongdoing. Notwithstanding their perpetrating the most heinous of crimes, they will feel not the slightest remorse. They plummet into cruelty and injustice which causes the heavens to tremble, and become subject to as blindness of heart and foolishness as to view their predicament normal.

Why on Earth?

Many tyrants throughout history, who saw themselves to be at the pinnacle of intellect, felt not the slightest discomfort with the atrocities that they perpetrated. This is because their tyranny was to them the shrewdest of actions.

In pre-Islamic Makka, for instance, fathers buried their baby daughters alive, amidst the silent cries of the infants which made their mothers' hearts bleed. If a master throttled his servant, he would never feel pangs of conscience, or the slightest feeling of remorse. Cutting firewood or a slave was to them one and the same. What is more, they saw all these atrocities as rather natural and as their legitimate right.

Ruler of the Huns, **Attila**, who set off from Central Asia's Karakum Desert and covered a distance of 7,000 kilometres to Central Europe and Rome, left nothing but blood, suffering and tears in his wake.

Hulagu, who drove toward Baghdad, drowned 400 thousand innocent Muslims in the Tigris River. On top of that, he was overcome by such hatred and savagery that he had countless precious handwritten works and manuscripts thrown into the waters of the Tigris, so much so that the Tigris flowed the colour of blood and ink for days. That tyrant too felt not the slightest qualms of conscience from this carnage.

Alexander's campaign from Macedonia all the way to India, as well as **Genghis** and **Timur**'s military victories are also of this same nature. The other thing they left behind was oppression, tears and dousing the lands in blood.

And taking a look at recent history – is not **Communism**, a man-made system built upon the bodies of roughly twenty million people, the projection of a brutal mental constitution. When evaluated from the perspective of right and truth, does not all this reveal a scene of savagery to make even the most bloodthirsty hyenas tremble?

Even if they see all these brutalities that are the shame of humanity as great successes, history ultimately documents them as horrendous persecutions spawned by worldly ambition and greed.

These individuals perhaps possessed an intelligence, capacity and shrewdness that bordered on genius; however, due to their being deprived of the guidance of Divine revelation and as they had not undertaken a process of self-purification, they turned all these opportunities into an instrument of evil. Their conscience was blinded and their feelings of compassion, mercy and pity were obscured. Even if they perpetrated savageries irreconcilable with human dignity, their intellect presented these to them as quite natural and even necessary.

All brutal dictators throughout history have always seen themselves to be right and always sought the error in others. Today, the persecution, killing and even massacre in Syria, Egypt and similar places is a clear case in point. With their intellects that they shut off to the Divine truths, those committing such atrocities see their actions as the cleverest of actions. They are being swept up into a heedlessness and folly as horrific as to ignore the fact that they are ultimately leaving behind a hideous wreck of humanity, that they have incurred the damnation of millions of innocents and that they have multiplied their own punishment in the Hereafter.

Such scenes can be seen in every period of history. Great Muslim jurist **Abu Hanifa** was offered the post of Chief Judge of Baghdad, the highest office after the caliphate. However, knowing that his legal rulings would be skewed by the tyrannical rulers in power and made an instrument of wrongdoing and that millions of people would be subjected to persecution as a result, Abu Hanifa declined this offer. However, the ruling elite who could not fathom the wisdom behind his declining their offer sentenced him to prison and had him lashed. But Abu Hanifa, the world's greatest jurist, settled for being subjected to punishment in custody, over the legal rulings of Islam being distorted.

As can be seen, human reason that is driven by worldly and temporal ambition is dragged into such an imbecility as not to be able to see its own errors. Such reason, no matter how great a mind it is in reality, cannot free itself of deviating into error and oppression.

The tyrants who deemed Abu Hanifa deserving of such persecution and who saw themselves to be justified in their actions disappeared into oblivion in the rubbish heap of history and even their names have been forgotten. Abu Hanifa, however, continues to live in hearts today, being remembered as the **Imam Abu Hanifa** of the *Ahl al-Sunna wa'l Jama'a* – the upholders of the Sunna and the community.

Sound Judgement

History attests to the fact that the Pharaoh, Nimrod, Attila, Alexander, Hulagu and their equals became enemies of all humanity with what they did. In contrast, **Mawlana Jalal al-Din al-Rumi** and similar friends of God who were kneaded with the effusion of revelation, attained 'sound judgement' and reached the source of friendship and love, became a channel of peace and mercy for humanity throughout their lives and even after their death. And they will each remain a friend of all humanity for all eternity.

Mawlana Jalal al-Din al-Rumi truly continues to live in hearts even seven centuries later. It is well known that Rumi's *Mathnawi* is one of the most read works concerning the human spirit in the United States and Europe, in addition to the seminal works of other Sufis. Moreover, UNESCO's announcing 2007 to be the year of Mawlana Jalal al-Din al-Rumi in honour of his 800th birthday is another noteworthy development in this regard.

As Mawlana Jalal al-Din al-Rumi lends weight to the criteria and principles of the Qur'an and Sunna, which elevate the human being as the honour of creation, he has been acclaimed in Western humanist circles.

That is to say, the letter of guidance, which that great friend of Allah wrote with sincerity centuries ago, resounds and inspires ardour throughout the world today. Holding up a mirror to the person's inner world, the *Mathnawi* assists them in coming to know themselves and finding a solution to their troubles. It enables spirits weighed down by a materialist mindset to attain peace and repose and is a means to their guidance to the path of truth, for even if a person reaches the summit of material prosperity and owns the entire worldly realm, they would not be able to fill the void which lack of wisdom causes in their soul, with anything else.

Mawlana Jalal al-Din al-Rumi indicates the truth that leads the human being to true happiness:

"(Know that) the wisdom which is born of (human) nature and phantasy (is) the wisdom which lacks the overflowing grace of the Light of Allah, the All-Glorious One. Your worldly philosophy only increases supposition

and doubt; only the wisdom of the Religion elevates the human being above the skies.

The ingenious rascals of (this) latter time have aggrandised themselves over the ancients;

The (apt) learners of cunning have burnt (consumed) their hearts (in study) and have learned feints and tricks;

They have thrown to the winds patience and altruism and self-sacrifice and generosity - (qualities) which are the elixir of (spiritual) profit."

Peace of Spirit: Submission to Wisdom

✓ The **Philosophers** have alleged that they can find the truth with the reason and emotion, which are limited and beset by myriad weaknesses, but have not been able to satisfy themselves or others through these means.

✓ The **theologians** have aimed to advance with the indispensable principles of human intellect, by means of reasoning and analogy, even if in the matter of Divine revelation. However, as they too have employed reason as a means, they have only been useful in matters only within its sphere of authority and have been deprived of any opportunity to appease spirits in matters beyond human intellect.

✓ As for the true **Sufis** on the path of the Qur'an and Sunna, they have continued to make headway beyond the point at which reason runs short, with their wings of wholehearted submission.

As a result of this surrender, they have drawn advantage from the horizons of **wisdom** and have been favoured with the manifestations of intimate knowledge of Allah. The human spirit can only attain true repose commensurate with their insight.

As 'Ali, may Allah be well pleased with him, has indicated:

"Put your spirits to rest with sayings and acts of wisdom, for spirits weary just as bodies do."

"Admonish the people with thought-provoking and wise counsel so that their hearts can achieve repose."

Wisdom, in the true sense of the term, is to be able to comprehend the mysterious reality of things and events.

Wisdom is to enable the intellect to grasp its incapacity in relation to perceiving truth and reality. Many mysteries that cannot be grasped with the intellect can be solved only with wisdom. The real meaning of the Divine manifestations in the universe can be read only with the eye of wisdom.

Were it not for **wisdom**, mysteries would have remained hidden. If secrets had not been revealed, hearts could not derive blessing from the climate of intimate knowledge, and such eminent personalities as **Mawlana Jalal al-Din al-Rumi, 'Abd al-Qadir**

Jilani, Yunus Emre, Shah al-Naqshband and Aziz Mahmut Hudayi, as exceptional models for the believers, could not have been raised.

The springs of wisdom can only become manifest in a heart that has been purified, or spiritually cleansed and developed. In this regard, the believer is under the training and spiritual tutelage of Allah and His Messenger and attains a sound heart to the degree to which they are able to purge their inner world of all other than Allah.

The ultimate aim of knowledge is to be able to deepen in wisdom. It is to be able to unravel the mysteries of the Divine art exhibited in the Qur'an, the universe and the human being. Moreover, it is to be able to understand the manifestations of Divine power and majesty present in every single particle.

For instance, the science of medicine is concerned with the stupendous systems that Allah has placed within the human body. The science of botany deals with the Divine laws Allah Almighty has placed within plant life. Wisdom, however, pertains to knowing the owner of all the principles and laws that all the sciences involve. This is because the object of knowledge is not to stockpile information in the mind, but for the heart to be able to perceive the mystery and wisdom within the true source of that knowledge. And this is possible only with the manifestation of Divine light in the heart.

Allah, exalted and glorified be He, declares:

"He grants the Wisdom to whomever He wills, and whoever is granted the Wisdom has indeed been granted much good. Yet none except people of discernment reflect and are mindful." (2:269)

Thus, only the Sufis who are the people of wisdom have been able to revive hearts by providing the most satisfactory solutions to humanity's problems, whether through the guidance they offered throughout their lives, or by means of the works they left behind.

Muhammad Hamidullah, one of the leading Muslim scholars of the previous century, states:

"I was raised a rationalist. My legal study and research caused me to reject everything that could not be cogently described and demonstrated. Of course I observe such religious obligations as the prescribed prayer and fasting not due to Sufi reasons but due to juristic ones. I say to myself:

'Allah is my Lord, my Owner. He has commanded me to perform these and so I must. Moreover, rights and responsibilities are interconnected. Allah has com-

89

manded me to observe these for my own benefit. In that case, I am obliged with showing gratitude to Him.'

Since the time I began living in Western society, in a city like Paris, I have observed with great astonishment that what drives Christians to accepting Islam is not the views of scholars of jurisprudence or theology but such Sufis as **Ibn 'Arabi** and **Mawlana Jalal al-Din al-Rumi**. I have also had personal experiences in this regard. When I was asked for an explanation concerning an Islamic matter, my response which was based on intellectual proofs failed to satisfy the inquirer; however, Sufi explanations were swift to bear fruit. I increasingly lost my power of influence in this regard.

I now believe that, as in the time of **Ghazan Khan** following **Hulagu**'s devastating invasions, what is now to serve Islam at least in Europe and Africa is **not the sword, nor the mind but purely the heart, or Sufism itself**.

After witnessing this, I began examining certain works written on the topic of Sufism. This opened the eye of my heart. I came to understand that the Sufism in the era of the Messenger of Allah and the path of the great Muslim Sufis is not preoccupation with words or meaningless pursuits; it is advancing upon the shortest path between the human being and Allah and seeking the path of character development.

A person seeks (to understand) the wisdom behind the duties placed upon their shoulders. Material explanations in a spiritual field lead us away from our goal. Only spiritual explanations can satisfy the human being.[31]

Thus, the most satisfying answers that human beings seek, in addition to intellectual analysis and analogical reasoning, issues forth from the language of the Sufis who are able to call out to hearts from the horizon of Divine wisdom.

This is because these individuals endowed with intimate knowledge of Allah are the interpreters of an intellect cultivated with Divine revelation and a heart rejoicing in the climate of friendship with God. They know full well that the contemplation of an intellect in the domain of carnal desire, under imposition by such diseases as pride and self-conceit and deprived of the guidance of a sound heart, will be diverted from its course and will lead the human being to a Satan-like depravity and deviance. This is precisely why **Mawlana Jalal al-Din al-Rumi** has said:

---

31. M. Aziz Lahbabi, *İslâm Şahsiyetçiliği*, Trans. I. Hakkı Akın, 114-115, footnote 8, Istanbul, 1972. This footnote is the text of the letter dated 27 September 1967 that Muhammad Hamidullah wrote to the translator. Also see, (Mustafa Kara, *Metinlerle Günümüz Tasavvuf Hareketleri*, 542-543.)

"Were Satan to have as much love as reason, he would not have fallen into his current predicament."

Indeed, the very first struggle of the intellect transpired against Allah Almighty, Who created and sustained it. And the fool in such a struggle was none other than Satan himself.

The world is full of devils rebelling against the Divine commandments. The whisperings of these devils may seem shrewdness to heedless human beings. Whereas the true human ingenuity and cleverness is their submission to Allah Who created them and being able to defend themselves against the guile of Satan.

Again, **Rumi** points to the importance of casting aside all doubt and questioning concerning the truths transcending the intellect's capacity and wholeheartedly surrendering to Allah and His Messenger:

"While the intellect is skilled in our worldly affairs, it is wanting, due to its very nature, when it comes to being a vehicle to truth, Divine mystery, or to experiential knowledge of Allah. A vehicle is required for this celestial journey and this is the heart, love, spiritual rapture and immersion."

Muhammad Iqbal figuratively illustrates that there is no other path to freedom from the impasses of the intellect than purification of the heart and spirit and unreserved submission to the Divine truths:

"One night, I heard the bookworm in my library lament to the moth:

'I have lived inside the pages of Avicenna's works and have seen many volumes of Farabi's works; But I am still unacquainted with the wisdom of life. My days are still as dark for lack of sun.'

Indicating his half-burnt wings, the moth replied most aptly:

'Look! I have set fire to my wings for this love.' And then he continued:

You cannot find this subtlety in a book. Warmth and ardour bring vitality to life, and it is love which gives it wings.'

In other words, by showing the bookworm its wings, the moth was actually trying to say:

'Save yourself from perishing in the blind alleys of this philosophy! Take flight with the Mathnawi's sea of meaning overflowing with love, ecstasy and spiritual effusion!'

So, in order to illuminate the intellect and heart, one must spin around the lights of truth that trickle from the Divine source like a moth, as it were, with an intense love and ardour and must serve others with great exertion. Freedom from the quagmires of the mind and attaining peace and happiness can only be realised through this means. The horizon of a person who merges a sound logic and inspiration in themselves, by refining the intellect and refining the heart, escapes the clutches of fleeting and carnal ambitions and opens to endlessness.

The Spirit's Wings of Love

A believer is in need of the boundless insight and discernment of Divine love in every phase of their life. Otherwise, the transition from shell to essence, form to truth and from appearance to character proves to be a very difficult one.

Our Persian teacher back in our Imam Hatip high school years, **Yaman Dede** (Abdülkadir Keçeoğlu, d. 1962) used to say:

"I have a strong belief in the following truth:

One needs two wings to soar – love and worship. Love without worship and worship without love is a single wing."

Since it is not possible to fly with only one wing, it is essential to experience both belief and one's life of worship with love. It is crucial to perceive and again observe all the stages of servanthood to

Allah with love. Only in this way can perfection be attained.

It is owing to this fact that the Companions, moving beyond all the mind's hang-ups of doubt and questioning concerning the Divine and Prophetic commandments, constantly said, **"We hear and we obey"**. Similarly, saying, **"May my father and mother be sacrificed for you, O Messenger of Allah,"** they gave up even their own lives without hesitation and in a complete sense of surrender in the way of the Messenger of Allah, upon him be peace and blessings.

When the Prophet, may Allah bless him and grant him peace, asked them who would deliver a letter to certain Kings and Emperor inviting them to accept Islam, the Companions wholeheartedly stepped forward without engaging in such introspective interrogation as to how they would travel all that way, whether they would have a steed and provisions, and exactly how they would pass through executioners to read this letter. Far from it, they exhibited great ardour and deference in applying to fulfil such a task for they were intimate knowers who progressed from **ordinary reason** (*'aql al-ma'ash*) to a **spiritual intelligence** (*'aql al-ma'ad*), as a direct result of Prophetic training. In other words, by cultivating their intellect with the Divine truths, they released it from being the conduit of mere passing, worldly and bodily interests, whilst making it a positive quality, which attaches importance on eternal life and strives in preparing for it.

This is why the Companions transformed the era in which they lived into an Age **of Happiness**, even if they spent their lives in material hardship, and thus became the fortunate believers who established a civilisation of virtue. Indeed, being moulded with hardship is one thing, while being ill at ease is another.

Some people are subjected to various material hardships but are at the peak of inner peace. Some people are buried under spiritual unrest and dissatisfaction, and become lost in the whirlpools of a heavy heart despite not having a material care in the world.

When we look at the community of the Age of Happiness, not a single case of psychological crisis is encountered among the Muslims. In no Prophetic Tradition or narration do we see any Muslim pose a question concerning a psychological disorder.

That is to say, the life of worship fulfilled with ardour and devoted reverence simultaneously served as a sort of spiritual healing for the believers with the inner peace that it offered. A belief in the afterlife diminished all worldly problems in their eyes and in their hearts. As they sought refuge in the All-

Powerful One and deepened in the consciousness and perception of belief, they found peace spiritually.

Praising the **Helpers** and the **Emigrants** in the Qur'an, Allah, glorified and exalted be He, holds attaining this horizon of love of belief, faithfulness, submission and obedience up as the epitome of servanthood for the entire Muslim community.

'May Reason be Sacrificed for Muhammad!'

We too must constantly engage in self-criticism as to the extent to which we are able to abandon our own vain desires and fancies as well the intellect's worldly and carnal considerations for the sake of Allah. Like all the Prophets and sincere communities struggling for the sake of Divine Unity and Oneness, we too must look carefully at how much we are able to shatter the idols within us so as to advance on the path of Truth. Accepting the Qur'anic verses and Prophetic Traditions without feeling the need to weigh them up within the narrow confines of the intellect, we must be able to say, **"We hear and we obey!"** with an ardour, rapture and surrender akin to that of the Companions, and, in the words of **Mawlana Jalal al-Din al-Rumi:**

"Sacrifice our intellect before Muhammad."

In the words of **Necip Fazıl:**

99

Say not you have eye, mind, thought but all of them eradicate!

What appears to you a desert is a lake if he says it is a lake!

My Herald, my Saviour, my Master, My Messenger!

I would spurn any standard, even life, that you contravenes.

In you is human being and society, in you is foundation and building.

Welcome is everything from you, what you have brought, taken away and proclaimed.

We should be able to express our surrender to the Pride of Creation in such a way.

Great Muslim scholar and thinker **Imam Ghazali,** may his secret be sanctified, states:

"By the time I had done with the science of philosophy –acquiring an understanding of it and marking what was spurious in it – I had realized that this too did not satisfy my aim in full and that the intellect neither comprehends all it attempts to know nor solves all its problems."[32]

32. Ghazali, *Munqiz min al-Dalal*, Kitap Dünyası Neşriyat, Istanbul 1984, 127-128.

Necip Fazıl Kısakürek describes Ghazali's being in between intellect and gnosis, as follows:

"*The towering figure of thought known as Hujjat al-Islam (Proof of Islam)... Just as he was to place all his scholarly, intellectual and rational pursuits to one side and incline towards true experiential knowledge, he said:*

'*I have seen that everything amounts to taking refuge in the spiritual profusion of the Prophet of Prophets and that everything else is but fable, misgiving and fantasy... Reason, however, is a nonentity... Only a frontier!*'

And this brilliant mind, the likes of which the world had not seen, extinguished all its questionings, sought sanctuary in the spiritual profusion of the Prophet of Prophets and thus found the boundless."[33]

It must not be forgotten that if a person attaches importance only to their intellect and falls into the heedlessness of virtually idolising and deeming it their sole compass of truth, they single-handedly choke up all their channels of spiritual perception. A reason that is the plaything of the carnal soul and the laughingstock of Satan darkens the heart and paralyses the spirit.

---

33. *Veliler Ordusundan,* Büyük Doğu Yayınları, Istanbul 1976, 213.

Mirror of Truth

It is imperative that every human being under-
goes spiritual training. For this, there is a need
for a mirror of truth that will enable them to
behold themselves, see their deficiencies and strive
to redress them.

This mirror is the people of piety, the scholars
and gnostics who earnestly follow the Qur'an and
the Sunna. Without the instruction and guidance
of these, the human being could not on their own
render their intellect sound, purge their carnal self of
vice, or purify their heart of spiritual diseases.

Rumi vividly states in his *Mathnawi*:

*It is the (Sufi) elder full of understanding, the
knower of the (mystical) Way, who digs a channel for
the (pure) streams of the Universal Soul.*

(Man) can never (by) himself, purify the stream; human knowledge becomes useful (only) from the knowledge possessed by God."

"Whoever has seen and known his own defects has galloped with ten horses in perfecting himself. For the one who carries a presumption about his own perfection is not flying toward the Owner of Majesty because of it.

O owner of pretense, there isn't a worse fault in your soul than the (high) opinion of (your) perfection."

This us why receiving instruction by the Qur'an and Sunna and viewing the Divine and Prophetic commandments with the harmony of mind and heart is necessary in order to be secure against the quagmires of the intellect.

The consequence of the intellect's reflecting upon the **Qur'an**, which is in effect a mirror to the **human being**, the **universe** and the realities contained within each, is akin to the unrefined minerals mined from the earth. It is a heart filled with the fervour of belief that processes these minerals, extracting and refining them.

The **heart** is the centre of emotion. The force and authority of a spiritually advanced heart which has purged itself of all other than Allah – expressed with the terms, '*hads, ilham* and *sunuhat*', meaning intuition, inspiration and occurrences to the heart respectively – and which combines the proofs offered by the intellect, enables the complete comprehension of truth. This is similar to the broken pieces of a vase being reassembled to reveal its original form.

The Qur'an is truly like a vast ocean in which one can delve proportional to the level of their heart. Just as one who cannot swim can only dabble about in shallow water, a proficient diver can dive to the depths of the ocean and see what those on shore cannot, observing various utterly different, strange and mystifying scenes, those who advance on the path of piety encounter a great many manifestations of wisdom in the Qur'an and become truly enlightened by it. In the same way that a person's head begins to spin when they look down a deep well, the perceptions of a heart deepening in the truths of the Qur'an open toward endlessness render the servant a traveller upon the path of utmost astonishment and propel them to receiving a share in experiential knowledge.

In short, perfect realisation of truth and goodness necessitates the training of the intellect with Divine revelation and a heart possessing refined belief stepping in at the point where the intellect runs short and thus making up for its deficiency by submission. One cannot pass through to the realm of infinite realities purely with reason and without a life of the heart and its spiritual perceptions.

Necip Fazıl's following words point to the functions of the **intellect** and **heart** in the perception of realities:

"Like a labourer carrying measuring instruments on its back, reason follows the intuition. Feeling comes before thought and when that comes, reason starts measuring. We perceive everything, all at once. This happens with intuition, not with the intellect. With the heart and spirit... The intellect follows the spirit and measures these with the quantitative tools and reasoning particular to it."[34]

Certain philosophers realising that the intellect is not sufficient on its own set about in search of other means on the path of investigating truth. Many philosophers have emerged who have sought solutions to their dilemmas at times with feeling, sometimes with intuition and occasionally verging upon the irrational.

One of these is the French philosopher **Henri Bergson** (d. 1941), who accepted intuition or the occurrences to the heart as a means to reaching truth. Hence he represents one of the exceptions among philosophers who held the intellect as a basis for their views.

---

34.   *Batı Tefekkürü ve İslam Tasavvufu*, 85-86.

However, just as spring cannot come with just a few flowers, one can still not expect satisfactory answers from philosophy, to satiate the human being's search for truth. What is more, as **Bergson** was not acquainted with Islam, he was not able to perfect his discovery, because the altered Gospel that he held in his hands and in which he professed belief was not of a protected status, as with the Qur'an.

Moreover, in the same way that those seeking truth by excluding revelation and relying solely upon reason have been dragged into varying deviations, those who have reached certain discoveries and inspirations as a result of disciplining (*riyada*) and striving (*mujahada*) divorced of the guidance of revelation, are face to face with the same danger. This is because whether their discoveries and inspirations are of Divine or diabolical origin is not distinguishable without the guidance of revelation.

This is the reason for **Imam Rabbani**'s cautioning as follows:

"The path of spiritual discipline (riyada) and striving (mujahada) is identical to the path of reasoning. Just as reason and thought does not allow us to find truth without the guidance of the Prophets, spiritual discipline and striving cannot ultimately enable us to reach Allah. As the Prophets have received the

trust from Allah via the agency of the angels, who are incapable of erring, their knowledge has been protected against Satanic intervention. For in declaring in reference to Satan, *'My servants - you shall have no authority over any of them, unless it be such as follow you being rebellious (against Me, as you are),'* (15:42) Allah has supported and confirmed His Prophets."[35]

---

35. *Maktubat,* v. III, Twenty Third Letter.

Academic Confusions

Despite all this, we most regrettably observe in our day that holding philosophy up as the most superior discipline and belittling revelation and Sunna-based disciplines has become fashionable amongst some so-called theologians.

A scholar of religion who has not read the philosophy of mortals is seen among these persons as inadequate and even ignorant.

Referring to philosophy as the "High Court of the disciplines," there is an effort to glorify it as though seeking to whitewash an inferiority complex.

Completely hollow accusations, whether intentional or benighted, are being thrown forward to the effect of claiming that revelation stifles the contemplation of the intellect.

Mawlana Jalal al-Din al-Rumi calls out to such people of heedlessness and ignorance, whatever their

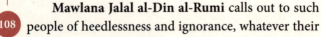

worldly position and scholarly status, and his call continues to resound today:

"If your sense of smell is awry, don't find fault with the rose."

In other words, he says, "If you cannot enter the Qur'an's atmosphere of reflection filled with infinite wisdom and truth, then at least don't fall into the heedlessness of blaming it and seek the problem in yourself."

However, it is easy to bring to reason someone who is aware of their ignorance. The difficult task is to bring ignorants who suppose themselves scholars who know everything, to reason. Indeed, **Said Nursi**'s reflections on this point are a clear demonstration of this fact:

"You know that if misguidance arises from igno-rance, it is easy to dispel. Whereas if it results from sci-ence and learning, it is difficult to eliminate. In former times, only one person in a thousand was in the latter category, and only one in a thousand such people would be reformed through spiritual guidance. For such people fancy themselves. They do not know, but they think they do know."[36]

---

36. Nursi, *The Words*, 752.

Providing the example of the scholars of the Children of Israel, Allah Almighty likens the situation of those poisoned with the arrogance of knowledge and dragged into ignorance with regard to temperament and morality, even if not with respect to knowledge, to **"a donkey carrying a load of books."**[37]

The scourge of historicism, yet another manifestation of the Western-based academic confusion that prioritises reason over revelation springing up in some faculties of theology, is another salient aspect of this matter.

Rejecting the 'universal' character of the Qur'anic verses, they call it into question. Claiming that the Divine commandments revealed in certain verses are particular to their time of revelation and ultimately regional – that they, in other words, are restricted to the Arabs and the Muslims living during the Age of Ignorance – they elicit a direful theological confusion.

Furthermore, by imagining themselves to possess an authority that Allah Almighty did not even confer upon His Beloved Messenger, they are being as presumptuous as to try to amend the unchanging commandments of the religion.

37.   See (62:5).

Indeed, Islam has allowed for the exercising of independent reasoning (*ijtihad*) with the rational and secondary proofs contained within the Qur'an and the Sunna, so as to respond to the needs of humanity before the changing conditions of the ages. This authority, however, is reserved solely for those scholars at the level of *mujtahid*, a qualified legal scholar possessing the capacity to deduce laws from the Qur'an and Sunna. However, there is no room for such independent reasoning in the presence of a clear verdict of the Qur'an and the Sunna. For instance, there can be no *ijtihad* in the matter of inheritance law, as explicit text exists in the sources in relation to it.

For the historicists, however, all these issues are open to debate. Their insolent heedlessness is reminiscent of the alterations of the Jews and Christians erstwhile in the texts of the Torah and Gospel.

The commandments and prohibitions of Islam have been determined in accordance with the unchanging peculiarities of human nature. These judgements are of a perfection that can respond to the requirements and needs of all time and space accessible to human beings from the Age of Happiness to the Last Day.

It is by virtue of this fact that the Qur'anic decrees do not grow old or lose their significance.

They forever preserve their perfection in relation to answering the needs of humanity in the best possible way. Consequently, claiming that a portion of the Qur'anic provisions are 'historical', or pertain to a given period and place, is an expression of misguidance bordering on unbelief.

By constantly sending Prophets as the structure of communities changed over time – with decrees pertaining to belief, however, remaining unchanged – Allah Almighty imposed new laws in accordance with the needs of the time. However, the Messenger of Allah, upon him be peace and blessings, is the Prophet sent until the end of time and no Prophet will come after him. That being so, the laws with which he was sent are of a nature that is able to respond to the needs of all humanity up until the Last Day.

Supposing otherwise is as tremendous a deviance as to ascribe incapacity to Allah Almighty, Who created humankind and therefore knows them better than they know themselves, and Who with His infinite knowledge, knows everything that has happened and is yet to happen. It is as grave a foolishness as Satan's entering into a dispute with Allah Almighty Who created him.

In this respect, there can be no absurd and futile an undertaking as to set out to debate the laws of Allah with the intellect bestowed by Allah Himself.

Those who fall into such a predicament ought to be reminded of the following verses of the Qur'an:

"(If those desert dwellers still insist on thinking themselves true believers,) say: 'What? Would you teach Allah (how truly you are devoted to) your Religion, while Allah knows all that is in the heavens and all that is on the earth?' Allah has full knowledge of everything."(49:16)

"...Then (like a people having no sense), do you believe in part of the Book, and disbelieve in part? What else, then, could be the recompense of those of you who act thus than disgrace in the life of this world? on the Day of Resurrection, they will be consigned to the severest of punishments. Allah is not unaware or unmindful of what you do."(2:85)

The Messenger of Allah, upon him be peace and blessings, has stated:

(Such a book is) the Book of Allah, glorified and exalted be He, (that it) secures the believers against every kind of trial (fitna). In it is information about what came before you, news about what will come after you and correct judgement for problems that arise between you. It is the Criterion (distinguishing between right and wrong), not a jest. Allah will crush any oppressor who abandons it and will misguide whoever seeks guidance from other than it..." (Tirmidhi, Fada'il al-Qur'an, 14/2906; Darimi, Fada'il al-Qur'an, 1)

No doubt all these trials which have emerged in our day in the religious sphere is glaring demonstration of what great ignorance the arena is filled with. The instigators of all this are those unfortunate souls who have not duly reflected upon the Qur'an or comprehensibly read the Qur'anic commentary and hadith canon in their entirety. Hence, they are not real scholars, but scholarly-looking individuals who have acquired an academic career via a superficial and incomplete reading and without having a sound grounding in the religious sciences. As for their professed views, these are the infelicitous expressions of the worldly admiration they feel for Western thought.

For if they had been adequately able to reflect upon the Qur'an and the hadith, they would have seen that the situation is not at all like they imagine. In fact, Allah Almighty invites us as His servants to reflect upon the Divine wisdoms and truths at 137 points throughout the Qur'an, in varying forms. What is more, it is not possible for a human intellect bereft of Divine revelation to reach the horizon of reflection that the Qur'an broadens for the human being even after thousands of years of reflection.

What is required of a Muslim scholar who is to guide humanity is deepening in contemplation, as well as a knowledge of such disciplines as the methods of intellectual reasoning and analogy, logic, mathematics, political science, ethics, sociology and psychology.

It is incumbent upon every Muslim scholar to learn the nature of the intellectual and philosophical currents of the day and to be able to educate themselves to the extent of being able to respond to the challenges of these from the perspective of Islam. Learning such ideas and struggling against them poses no threat to a belief which is firmly rooted in contemplation of the Qur'an and the Sunna.

On the contrary, a Muslim who has attained a realisation of truth will better comprehend the value and resplendence of Islam as they see the weaknesses of other worldviews. This, in turn, will serve to strengthen their faith, for truth becomes more clearly understood with its opposite.

Necip Fazıl says:

"The best belief, as stated by Muhyi'd-Din Ibn 'Arabi, is that which is attained after seeing the source of unbelief. Understanding the source of unbelief is incumbent upon every (perfected) believer... That is to say, saying, "I'm against communism," is not enough. You have to understand it..."[38]

A skilled diver can gaze upon magnificent scenes by swimming fearlessly in deep waters. There is no harm in a refined believer wandering through the cultures of seventy-two nations, like a compass needle, so

---

38.   *Batı Tefekkürü ve İslam Tasavvufu*, 69.

long as one of their feet remains firmly in the Divine law. What is objectionable is for one who cannot swim to dive into deep water. In other words, it is a person who has not properly processed the Qur'an and Sunna deeming the Western ideas embellished with powerful dialectical technique to be truth when they come across them, or at the very least, their feeling an admiration for such ideas.

Imam Ghazali's warning in relation in this respect is noteworthy:

"'Do not seek for the truth by means of men; find first the truth and then you will recognise those who follow it.' This is the procedure followed by a wise man. Once in possession of the truth he examines the basis of various doctrines which come before him, and when he has found them true, he accepts them without troubling himself whether the person who teaches them is sincere or a deceiver. Much rather, remembering how gold is buried in the bowels of the earth, he endeavours to disengage the truth from the mass of errors in which it is engulfed.

The skilled coin-assayer plunges without hesitation his hand into the purse of the coiner of false money, and relying on experience, separates good coins from bad. It is the ignorant rustic, and not the experienced assayer, who will be cheated by a false coiner. The unskilled *swimmer must be kept away from the seashore, not the expert in diving...*

As a matter of fact, men have such a good opinion of themselves, of their mental superiority and intellectual depth; they believe themselves so skilled in discerning the true from the false, the path of safety from those of error, that they should be forbidden as much as possible the perusal of philosophic writings..."[39]

As can be seen from these statements, one of the greatest harms of preoccupation with philosophy is an inability to recognise the fallacies mixed in with the truths of philosophical views, supposing these to be true also and being thus dragged into theological error. And so, in making their evaluation on Islam, the Orientalists of our time package and present a single falsehood with ten truths in order to spread their fallacious ideas. Owing to this strategy, they toy with the belief of those who possess insufficient knowledge about Islam or who are deprived of a depth of piety.

On no account can the fewness of these false notions, whether coming from the Orientalists or from the philosophy flank, allow them to be excused. For their giving rise to any doubt or hesitation concerning a Divine decree connected with belief is more than enough harm for the individual.

39.　Ghazali, *Munqiz min al-Dalal*, Kitap Dünyası Neşriyat, Istanbul 1984, 125.

This is because belief does not allow for fragmentation. That is, it cannot be reduced to components, fragments, or parts and is valid only as a single whole. There is no difference in terms of the end predicament that a person will face in the event of their denying the Qur'an in its entirety or just a single ordinance. Both situations will divest a person of their belief.

As a result of this danger, it has been viewed as detrimental for Muslims other than those qualified scholars who are able to acutely distinguish between truth and falsehood to be engaged with such fallacious ideas.

In contrast, the preoccupation with such disciplines of enlightened, intellectual Muslim scholars with a sound understanding of the Qur'an and Sunna who are able to uphold Islam in the face of its enemies, with a view to protecting the people from the false ideas and claims to come from philosophy, cannot be disparaged. Far from it, this is a binding obligation for them. Furthermore, what is required is to educate and train Muslim scholars who are experts in the field of philosophy so as not to leave the field to the monopoly of atheist and materialist philosophers.

Imam Ghazali himself also studied this science within the framework of defending *Ahl al-Sunna* belief and struggling against groups who corrupted the belief of the people. Ghazali even engaged in thorough investigation and inquiry philosophy and learned all of its principles with a view to preventing such accusations to come from philosophers as, "One is an enemy of what one doesn't know". After authoring the work *Maqasid al-Falasifa* (Doctrines of the Philosophers), which dealt expressly with all the philosophical matters of the day, he penned his *Tahafut al-Falasifa* (Incoherence of the Philosophers) criticising these. In particular, Ghazali expounded the divergence of Aristotle and three of his followers from *Ahl al-Sunna* belief in twenty points, denouncing them as unbelievers in three of these.

Another danger of preoccupation with philosophy is the attempt to establish Islamic thought upon a philosophical foundation – a malady brought about by blind admiration for the West. It is predicating one's views upon the intellect and minimising scripture, whether deliberately or unwittingly.

Whereas Islam is in no need whatsoever of synthesis with man-made systems, currents of the present age, or for that matter, with other religions. Seeing a need for this is a failure to duly recognise the resplendence of Islam, for Islam is the religion of truth and possesses the most perfect worldview. In eras and societies where it was properly practised, it has always been a source of peace and harmony.

To suggest that a nightingale, noble and perfect in all respects, is able to sing so melodiously by taking the cacophonous crow as its example and that it would not be able to preserve this quality and beauty without that crow, is but an ignorant absurdity.

In an article entitled, **"Seeking a New World Order and the Islamic Civilisation,"** Rector and Chairman of the Islamic University of Rotterdam, Professor Ahmet Akgündüz, makes the following observations concerning the role of Islam as the single worldview that will bring peace to all humanity:

*"In our day, where all **ism's** – communism and capitalism and their illegitimate descendants first and foremost – have gone bankrupt and where their bankruptcy has been announced by their theoreticians themselves, there is no serious alternative civilisational order to ensure the happiness of humanity other than Islam.*

A concrete example of this is a secret meeting held by priests in Rome and the decisions taken herein. In this secret meeting, the priests admitted that in Italy, the Western European country most affected by the scourge of communism, the youth who turned away from communism no longer believed in the principles of an altered Christianity, that they perhaps sought the true religion that is the natural religion of humankind, and that as a result of this earnest search, sixty percent of them discovered Islam.

120

Let me state at once, that if we Muslims can put forth the true Islam and the righteousness that Islam deserves with our words and way of life, this rate of acceptance would increase further.

Those in the West fearing precisely this are exerting great effort to misrepresent Islam to their own generations in order to stop this gravitation to Islam.

Let me state right at this point that a people without a religion cannot survive. Christian societies that were swept up by the winds of communism, especially Russia, and whose belief systems were thus shaken cannot turn back to Christianity. The place to which they are headed, provided that we fulfil our obligation, is Islam."

That people in the West are surrounded by a dense fog of bigotry due to centuries-old negative preconditioning against Islam and that because of this they are unable to adequately benefit from the light of Islam and are thus forced to make do with the flickering candlelight they hold in their hand was mentioned earlier.

Incidentally, I should also add that such smear campaigns to the effect of, "Islam is a tribal religion and Muslims are wild and savage people," levelled against Islam for centuries in order to prevent the gravitation towards Islam have been replaced today by the lie and calumny that, "Islam is a religion of terror and war". And in support of these allegations, they show the deplorable condition of Muslim nations writhing under war, anarchy, poverty and backwardness as evidence.

Whereas they hide from their masses the fact that the seeds of sedition they themselves sowed for the realisation of their own colonialist schemes have had an enormous role to play in the formation of these conditions. Nonetheless, as these realities cannot be hidden in this communication age, as they were previously, the number of those who see the truth for what it is, is increasing with each passing day.

It is not possible for a right-minded individual who is able to consider Islam fairly and without any negative preconditioning to accept it to be a religion of terror and savagery as is claimed, for the twenty-three year Prophethood of **Allah's Messenger** is, in a sense, a struggle against terrorism. It is comprised of the effort to eradicate all the atrocities committed against human beings, animals and the environment. The Pride of Humanity, the Seal of the Prophets, upon him be peace and blessings, delivered truth, law and justice to all humanity.

Thus, one of the leading figures who prepared the intellectual groundwork for the 1789 French Revolution, **Lafayette**, examined all legal systems prior to the publication of the famous 'Declaration of the Rights of Man and of the Citizen'. Upon seeing the superiority of Islamic law, he could not help but proclaim, *"O Muhammad! No other has ever been able to attain the level you have reached in the realisation of justice..."*

Indeed, the Age of Ignorance in which the sun of humanity and virtue set and where the whole world was enveloped by the darkness of unbelief and immorality, witnessed the dawn of truth and felicity with his arrival and his honouring it with his presence.

The Bedouin deserts, the formidable rivers of blood in which infant girls were buried alive and brethren tribes slaughtered each other, were transformed into luminous gardens of civilisation with the message and guidance of that Prophet of Mercy.

The swamps of hostility, conflict and blood feuds had but all dried up and the peaceful and love-filled climate of religious fellowship entered into. An unequalled **civilisation of virtue** that humanity still looks upon with envy was thus established.

Such a light of guidance is Islam that it elevates communities that duly hold fast to it to the peak of humanity, virtue and civilisation throughout all time and in every place. Just as a more perfect way of life than Islam, which transforms worldly life into a garden of Paradise, has not existed until now, it will not exist hereafter.

For this reason, properly comprehending the splendour of Islam as the sole religion of truth upon the earth today, holding fast to it and representing it in the best possible way with our manner and conduct is the duty of all of us as Muslims.

While humanity has been unable to find what it seeks in distorted and man-made religions or philosophies and has been dragged into spiritual crisis and dissatisfaction, there can be no confusion as direful as the adherents of Islam feeling an enthusiasm and admiration for these misguided paths.

I would like to relate an anecdote here:

Years ago, the famous French philosopher, politician and former member of the French Communist Party **Professor Roger Garaudy** had come to Istanbul after investigating Islam and becoming Muslim. He was speaking at a conference at Yıldız Palace where I too was present. Addressing his audience, Garaudy said:

"You (as Muslims) are sound in (terms of) thought. The West, however, is afflicted in every respect. But how strange it is that you imitate the ill-stricken and are oblivious to your own health and soundness."

While, in our day, philosophical and intellectual currents should be analysed with respect to an Islamic standpoint and worldview in faculties of theology providing graduate studies in Islamic studies, the fact that some individuals have instead condescended to criticising Islam through the lens of these philosophical and intellectual movements is yet another manifestation of this warped mindset.

Moreover, the fact that many students are urged to learn erroneous ideas without having a solid grounding in the religious sciences beforehand, or without an adequate knowledge of the Qur'an and Sunna, is a situation that poses a risk of misleading young minds and leading them astray. Not all students of theology are an **Imam Ghazali** in order for them to realise what significant weaknesses those views have instead of being shaken by the false views they analyse, and for them to thus reinforce their belief.

Outside the few exceptions, it is very difficult to indicate a Muslim who has increased in piety or devoutness as a result of their studies in philosophy. But many Muslims undertaking study in philosophy without knowledge and gnosis who develop an attitude of aversion to religion can readily be found.

For this reason, if philosophy must be taught, then students must first be provided a satisfactory background in Qur'anic and Sunna studies, and instruction in philosophy must be offered by evaluating not just its positives but its negatives also. As philosophical ideas are imparted, the way in which Islam responds to those ideas must be demonstrated with convincing arguments and proofs. That is to say, theories which constitute contradiction with Islamic truths, especially atheistic and materialistic theories, must be expounded along with their antitheses. In this way, Islam's being the sole worldview that is able to provide satisfying solutions to the philosophical dilemmas faced by humanity, must be set forth.

The ideal human type intended throughout Islam's history, in the **Nizamiyya**, **Iznik** and **Fatih** *madrasas*, was the scholarly personality who possessed as extensive a knowledge background as to be able to offer guidance to the community in every field. In other words, after deepening in such Islamic sciences as Qur'anic commentary, hadith, classical theology, jurisprudence and Sufism, the Muslim scholar could acquire knowledge in law, or medicine, or philosophy, as conditions and competence would permit.

It is well known, however, that at the present time, an education at such a level is no longer aspired to and deepening in only a given discipline has been adopted. Furthermore, it becomes clear that in our day students graduate from certain faculties of theology without even a sufficient grounding in the Qur'anic and hadith sciences. Expressed differently, the education provided in Islamic studies is far from the ideal.

For instance, it is self-evident how small a space studies of *Sirat al-Nabi*, or the life of Allah's Messenger who is a living commentary of the Qur'an and Sunna, occupies in the curricula of theology faculties. And such studies, on top of that, go no further than being the mere sum of chronological facts.

Whereas *Sirat al-Nabi*, the Life of the Prophet, is a subject that needs to be analysed and understood in-depth, with respect to the character of Allah's Messenger, upon him be peace and blessings, alongside his biography.

Allah Almighty commands us to seek refuge in Him in each unit of the prayer with the entreaty, **"Guide us to the Straight Path."** (1:6) In expounding, as it were, what is meant by the Straight Path, Allah declares, directly addressing His Messenger, **"You are indeed one of the Messengers (commissioned to convey Allah's Message); upon a straight path."** (36:2-4) In that case, each and every Muslim aspiring to reach the Straight Path with which The Almighty is well-pleased is obligated to be closely acquainted with the Messenger of Allah and to follow in his luminous footsteps.

The Qur'an is one of the fundamental sources for Muslims, while the life of the Prophet, the Fine Exemplar (*al-uswa al-hasana*), upon him be peace and blessings, is another. Allah Almighty has revealed His commandments in brief in the Qur'an, while He has exhibited the particulars and praxis of these in the exemplary life of His Messenger, upon him be peace and blessings. It is for this reason that a Qur'anic verse declares:

"He who obeys the Messenger (thereby) obeys God..." (4:80)

In another Qur'anic verse, Allah says of His Beloved Messenger:

"You are surely of a sublime character, and do act by a sublime pattern of conduct." (68:4)

As a result, those seeking the most perfect of conduct must strive to understand the exemplary character of Allah's Messenger. All the Islamic sources filling the libraries over the past 1400 years have been penned to described one Book, the Qur'an, and a single person – the Prophet Muhammad, upon him be peace and blessings, who was presented to humanity as a living and breathing model of the Qur'anic conduct.

Again, a Qur'anic verse declares:

"The Trustworthy Spirit brings it down on your heart, so that you may be one of the warners (entrusted with the Divine Revelation), in clear Arabic tongue." (26:193-195)

Hence, a believer who seeks to adequately grasp the Qur'an must be familiar with the inner world of the Messenger of Allah as his twenty-three year Prophethood serves as a commentary of the Qur'an. The mysteries and wisdoms the Qur'an can only be understood by means of benefiting from the spiritual tapestry of Allah's Messenger, upon him be peace and blessings.

In this respect, understanding him is the most important step on the path of servitude to Allah. Without understanding him, knowing him, following in his footsteps and receiving a share in his spiritual sensibility, neither will our belief be a complete belief, nor will we be able to fully comprehend the Qur'an, nor will our servanthood be a perfect one.

Without the life of the Messenger of Allah, may Allah bless him and grant him peace, being known, none of the Islamic sciences – Qur'anic commentary, hadith, jurisprudence or ethics and morality – can be properly understood. For this reason, *Sirat al-Nabi* heads the list of the most important subjects to be given weight to for an accurate understanding of Islam.

Furthermore, Allah Almighty frequently gives examples of the distinctive qualities of His Prophets and Messengers in His Book. Informing us of the solutions offered by the Prophets to the problems faced in their communities, He wills for us to thoroughly analyse and reflect upon these, and take these as an example. In this respect, the chain of Prophethood being taught alongside the history of religions is essential in today's theology faculties.

A student of theology must be equipped with this foundational knowledge first and foremost in order for them to later endeavour to benefit from the other disciplines commensurate with their capacity and means.

For this reason, those who are to acquire the Islamic sciences must first completely consolidate the foundations of their belief in the horizon of reflection opened by the Qur'an and the Sunna. While they remain far from contemplation of the Qur'an and belief does not adequately take root in their hearts, they lose strength and are driven away by the first storm. This is one of the most significant problems leading those encountering erroneous ideas embellished with reason and the principles of logic astray.

May Allah Almighty enable us all to duly appreciate the Qur'an and Sunna, allow our reason and heart to deepen in contemplation of these two

sources and benefit from the Divine wisdoms contained therein.

May he grant us a refined and wakeful heart which trembles with the manifestations of Divine power and majesty in the Qur'an, the universe and the human being.

May He enable us to derive benefit from the Divine decree, "Read in and with the Name of your Lord, who has created," (96:1) and grant us a sound reason and heart that senses the Artist through the art and the Maker through every single thing they see.

Amin...

TABLE OF CONTENTS

Table of Contents

....
....
....
....
....
....
....
....
....
....
....
....
....
....
....
....
....
....
....
....
....
....
....
....
....
....
....
....
....

....
....
....
....
....
....
....
....
....
....
....
....
....
....
....
....
....
....
....
....
....
....
....
....
....
....
....
....